THE WOOD

THE WOOD

An Outline of Christianity

C.S.M.V.

With a Foreword by
Bishop Neville Talbot, D.D.

*An highway shall be there and a way ... called
the way of holiness . . . the wayfaring men,
though fools, shall not err therein.*

W. HEFFER & SONS LTD.
CAMBRIDGE

First published in 1935

PRINTED AND BOUND IN GREAT BRITAIN
AT THE WORKS OF
W. HEFFER & SONS LTD.
CAMBRIDGE, ENGLAND

TO

GRACE,

WHO ASKED FOR IT;

AND TO

ALL THE FRIENDS

WHO IN VARIOUS WAYS ENCOURAGED IT,

INCLUDING

ONE,

WHO HELPED UNKNOWINGLY.

FOREWORD

I LOOK upon this book as a very spirited and able endeavour to draw, with sweeping strokes, an Outline of Christianity; and I feel honoured by being asked to write a short Foreword to it. The range of the book is enormous—the author herself calls it an "impossible book"—but that only heightens one's sense of her courage and width of mind. A willingness to be hospitable to the new light, which has been thrown on the whole story of man and upon the Bible in particular by modern science and scholarship, is evident at the outset. There is a most attractive feeling of glow in writing and a real sparkle of wit and humour. While the effort 'to see the Wood' has inevitably meant the making of broad and bold generalizations, yet there is much delicate perception of detail and particulars, which is undoubtedly the fruit of lovingly devout meditation and of intimate communion with God in Christ.

I must not be taken to endorse all and everything contained in this far-ranging endeavour. I have wondered whether the author might not have been satisfied with the ground covered by the Bible; for it is her brave and sure-footed treatment of Scripture which has most kindled my admiration. But I respect her desire to grapple with the whole and not only with a part of 'the Wood.' I think that the book is calculated to be of especial help to those who join together in Study Circles, and to reproduce in their discussions some of its range and vitality. I believe, too, more generally, that it will help many, who are among 'the trees' and are lost in them, to reach a height whence they can discern 'the Wood.' So may it be.

✠ NEVILLE S. TALBOT,
Bishop.

NOTTINGHAM,
July, 1935.

vii

WANTAGE,
FEAST OF THE ANNUNCIATION, 1935.

For a person unknown and unqualified to put forth a book on so vast a subject as Christianity demands both explanation and apology.

It came about on this wise. In 1922 the reading of Hendrik van Loon's *Story of Mankind* gave me for the first time a vision of History *as a whole*, and made me realise also that the crying need of most of us Christians is a similar unification of our outlook on Theology. It was not until ten years later, when long search had failed to find any *one* book to meet this need, that in response to a clear lead followed by a chain of compelling circumstances I sat down to write it myself. The task has proved both heartbreaking and enthralling; the result of course is inadequate, and I can only echo the hope expressed by the editors of the *New Commentary*, that the book may be found 'not perfect but useful,' until someone else is raised up to write a better one.

Where everything is owed, adequate acknowledgment, either to books or persons, is impossible. For the doctrinal backbone of the book I am, however, supremely indebted to Dr. N. P. Williams' Bampton Lectures on *The Ideas of the Fall and of Original Sin*, to Fr. Thornton's great work, *The Incarnate Lord*, and to *Essays Catholic and Critical*, edited by Dr. Selwyn. As to those who have helped me personally, their name is legion: never had inexperienced author more or better friends. They are all included in the dedication, but three names must be mentioned: the Rev. L. A. C. Allen, Subwarden of C.S.M.V., without whose encouragement at the outset the book would never have been begun; Dr. Kidd, Warden of Keble and of C.S.M.V., whose pupil I was once privileged to be and to whom I owe, besides much invaluable oral teaching, a constructive criticism of the rough draft in 1933; and finally my cousin, the Rev. A. J. Winnington-Ingram who in 1934 gave me courage and counsel for the final revision.

The design on the cover is based upon a little picture which, with the words beneath it, 'floated in one day,'— so he himself accounted for it,—to the Rev. B. S. Lombard. It had been long in my possession, and the title of this book quite independently chosen, when the kinship of his thought to mine suddenly came home to me. I am very grateful for his permission to make use of it. Finally, I would thank the artist, whose tailpieces express three of the book's main ideas far better than do any words of mine.

THE AUTHOR.

CONTENTS

xii CONTENTS

CHAPTER I

GENERAL INTRODUCTION

Most people receive and collect their intellectual knowledge of Christianity under four headings,—Old Testament, New Testament, Doctrine and Church History. Old Testament means the rather tangled history of the people from whom Our Lord was born, but as it leaves off some centuries before His Birth the New Testament opens against a background for which the Old has only very partially accounted. Still more is it difficult to fit in the troubled world and divided Church of history and of our own times with the glowing language of the New Testament about Our Lord's conquest of evil, with the apparently quite ideal community of the first days after Pentecost and with the vision of the New Jerusalem with which the Bible ends. And Doctrine, which is usually taken to mean creeds and catechisms, is couched in language which seems to hang midway between the Bible and our own experience, lacking vital contact with either.

Nobody who really cares is satisfied with this four-compartment system, but the English custom of taking it politely for granted that practising Christians know what they believe makes it difficult for people who have no opportunity for wide theological study to remedy their defect, and they therefore continue regretfully unable to see the Wood for the Trees.

This book is an attempt both to see the Wood itself as a whole and to view it in relation to what lies around and beyond it. It is like going up in an aeroplane to get a bird's eye view which, once seen, will always be present in mind when one walks afterwards among the Trees. To do this, the four subjects must be treated as one, or perhaps it is truer to say that Doctrine, by which is meant God's progressive Self-revelation to man, must be regarded as the thread on which the other three are strung, since it is Doctrine in that sense which makes Old Testament, New Testament and Church History a unity. For Christianity is primarily the religion of *revelation*. Religion means literally *that which binds*, faith which rules life; and to reveal or make a revelation means to show something by drawing back the veil or curtain which hides it. So revealed religion means that a personal God makes known to men things which they could not otherwise have known, and elicits their faith and love and obedience in response.

From this point of view Christianity can be considered under the three headings: *Creation; Fall* or *Counter-creation; Restoration* or *Re-creation*. By Restoration is meant here God's persistence in His purpose for the universe after the entrance into it of sin. No single word really expresses the twofold idea of putting right the wrong and fulfilling the original purpose; but this, in spite of its usual and more limited uses in history, seems on the whole to be the best. Under it, human history has to be considered in three periods. The first is the period of Preparation, which centred latterly in the Chosen People; the second is the Incarnate Life of Our Lord on earth; and the third, which may be called the Last Days, is the period since Pentecost, in which God's instrument is the Christian Church, and in which we ourselves are living. These Last Days will end with the Second Coming of Our Lord, so that our final task will be to consider the as yet unfulfilled prophecies of the consummation of the Restoration which His Second Coming will introduce,— a consummation the confident expectation of which is no pious extra but integral to Christian faith.

There are a few points about revelation which need to be made clear. In the first place it is in one sense universal. Behind and around God's special revelation to the Chosen People lies His more general *praeparatio evangelica* of the whole world, whose ultimate bringing to the knowledge of revealed truth was the purpose of Israel's chosenness; and in the same way He is ever at work among those at present outside the Christian Church. Secondly, the focus of revelation is the individual. Even among the most primitive peoples, where the clan counts for everything, it is always through the individual that revelation gets in. Men make contact with God as units, not as clans, and the clan's religion is based upon the pooled and to some extent formulated experience of its individual members. Men being what they are, there is always an element of misinterpretation and a tendency to restrict and minimize the truth in one direction or another even in revealed religion proper; while in non-Christian systems gleams of truth may be combined with much that is its very negation. But the fact remains that Theology, that is, men's theories about God, *is based on their experience of God;* and, as with all other sciences, because the experience is continuous, no theory will permanently hold the field which proves inadequate to that experience at its highest. See it in history: Abraham draws from a strange spiritual contact the conclusion that God is to be trusted; and on that rock is built the faith of his descendants; Hosea, taught by his own domestic tragedy, becomes the first exponent of God's forgiving love; Isaiah, having once seen His holiness, spends his life proclaiming the obligations which it entails; Peter companies with Jesus and learns to call Him Christ; the centurion watches Him die and names Him a son of God. So Theology is born.

Finally, because Theology is based on experience, only those who have experience are competent to understand it. People who reject the Christian creed but do not live the Christian life are like those who, having never looked down a telescope, deny the existence of the heavenly wonders which the telescope reveals. *Expertus novit credere:** he who has tried knows how to believe; and for such only is this book.

*A quotation from the Rosy Sequence, *Jesu dulcis memoria*, of S. Bernard.

CHAPTER II

INTRODUCTION TO THE OLD TESTAMENT

THE progressive Self-revelation of God to the Chosen People which is chronicled in the Old Testament was received by individuals through whom it became the possession of the nation. The Nicene Creed sums this up by saying that God the Holy Ghost 'spake by the prophets.'

Two matters essential to our understanding of the Old Testament are here contained,—Prophecy and Inspiration.

The word prophet means literally a forthteller, and is used to translate the Hebrew *nābhî'*, plural *nebhî'îm*, the root meaning of which is a commissioned speaker. This word is applied in scripture not only to such men as Samuel, Elijah and the writing prophets, but also to Abraham, Moses and David. It is an old word filled with a new meaning, for Hebrew prophecy had a humble origin. All Semitic peoples had their *nebhî'îm*, such as were the prophets of Baal on Mount Carmel, who withstood Elijah and worked themselves into a frenzy with knife-cuts. Ecstatic fervour of this kind is the chief feature of this type of prophecy; you may see it in pilgrims to Mecca to-day, or read of it in Virgil's wonderful description of the Cumaean Sibyl. Its chief characteristic is that the prophet can only function when his personality is in abeyance; he is a medium rather than an intermediary. It is probable that the 'sons of the prophets' mentioned in the books of Samuel and Kings were prophetic Guilds of this type existing in Israel side by side with the prophets of the higher sort and, as it appears, but little esteemed though not without their uses. The process of evolution was slow. Elijah indeed towers above the *nebhî'îm* on

Carmel, yet Isaiah and Jeremiah calmly and faithfully maintaining their vocation are nobler than Elijah.

This development of Hebrew prophecy is in accordance with a great principle. Again and again in history we see God taking some crude, faulty human institution, and gradually transmuting it. It is the method symbolised in Our Lord's first miracle, the method by which fallen humanity itself is now in process of restoration and renewal.

The primary concern of the Hebrew prophets was with the sins and needs of the present. First and foremost their work was to interpret history and to preach righteousness. But on two recurrent occasions the forthteller becomes also the foreteller,—when the urgency of Israel's unrepentance leads him to predict the approach of judgment, and when his message concerns the promised intervention of God in human history. For the Chosen People, unlike all others, looked for their Golden Age to the future.

The subject of prophecy brings us to that of Inspiration. To inspire means to breathe into. The doctrine of Inspiration, as we have now come to understand it, is the formulation of experience both Hebrew and Christian; and in regard to the Old Testament it may be summarised as follows.

God the Holy Spirit inspired certain people to write, and others to edit the documents which came in time to constitute the Old Testament; and He also guided the selection of those particular books as the Canon or Rule of Scripture. In this work of inspiration He did not sweep aside the personalities of His agents, but worked through them; so that the inspired writer was not a machine but a conscious, willing co-operator with Him Who inspired. The message thus conveyed may, and often does, mean far more than the messenger could possibly have known: it is God's message, yet it comes to men coloured by the messenger's personality, environment and outlook.

Mistakes of the kind that spring from the limitation of human knowledge are therefore not precluded by the fact that the writer was inspired. There are plenty of them in the Old Testament; but the Holy Spirit Who inspires is guarantee that they are not vital. Once again it is the principle declared at Cana. God takes men as He finds them, and, if they let Him, makes them something better, instruments of His redemptive purpose. And beyond all doubt it is better to be a man than a type-writer, even if the type-writer is more accurate than the man.

The Old Testament is most truly a unity, for it is the record of the one revelation; but the record was made 'by divers portions and in divers manners,' and many helped both to receive and to record it. The literature of the Old Testament therefore requires skilled investigation. The Greek word for a literary expert is a *critic;* and literary criticism is of two kinds, Higher or documentary, and Lower or textual.

The Higher Criticism of the Old Testament has rendered untold service to Theology, because it has enabled us to trace the *development* of revelation; and some knowledge of its conclusions is indispensable. The first five books of the Bible, known as the Pentateuch, or in the Jewish Canon 'the Law,' are as it were a single rope woven of four strands, four documents of different dates put together by later editors. The oldest of these four is the narrative known, as is its author, by the symbol J, because its name for God consists of the four consonants JHVH, probably to be pronounced Jahveh or Yahweh, though more familiar to us as Jehovah.*

* The form Jehovah arose from the combination of the consonants JHVH with the vowel sounds of *'Adōnai,* Lord. Intense reverence for the Divine Name led the Jews in later times to abstain from pronouncing it; another title, Adonai or 'Elōhîm, was substituted in reading, and the original pronunciation was lost. The form Jehovah was devised in the 16th century for convenience; while Jahveh is the attempt of modern scholars to reconstruct the original.

The second document is known as E, because it prefers the divine title *'Elōhîm*. It is probable that J was written in the ninth century B.C. in Judah, and E somewhat later in Israel; but both incorporate much earlier oral tradition, whose accuracy they had no means of checking; and even quote from earlier written sources, such as the Book of Jashar. These two documents were subsequently combined, and are therefore not always distinguishable. Together they form what is called the *Prophetic* narrative, because they reflect the period when the religious interest of Israel centred in the prophets, though earlier than the prophets who left their message in writing. The document D, of which the main part of the Book of Deuteronomy consists, may be identified for the most part with the Law book found in the Temple which occasioned Josiah's reformation. Thus it dates from the seventh century in Judah, and probably owes much to the influence of Amos and Hosea. It consists chiefly of discourses put into the mouth of Moses, which set forth the laws for life and worship to be observed in Israel. One of its chief features is insistence on their being but *one* sanctuary for Jahveh-worship; and from this Deuteronomic standpoint the books known by the Jews as 'the Former Prophets,'—namely, Joshua, Judges, Samuel and Kings, were subsequently edited.

Lastly there is P, the *Priestly* narrative. This dates from the Exile in the sixth century B.C., when the only hope of restoration to the land of promise seemed to lie in faithfulness to worship and the ceremonial Law. P therefore gives a comprehensive survey of the ground covered by J and E, starting with the Creation and giving special attention to the origin of religious institutions. But in doing this he reads back into the earlier history the standpoint of his own time; and treats of Abraham and Moses as though they too had lived in the sixth century. Finally, somewhere in the fourth century B.C., after sundry previous editings these four documents were combined in their present form by a redactor known by the symbol R^JP. But an ancient eastern historian employed his sources far otherwise than we do to-day. The modern writer reads, and then reproduces in his own words; if he quotes he shows it by inverted commas: R^JP and his like sat down with all their sources in front of them and copied from them one after the other, with occasional insertions of their own. That is why the Pentateuch is a patchwork of duplicate narratives, different styles and legal codes,—J, E, D and P have one apiece,—each reflecting a different historical background.

These facts have been given as briefly as possible, with no discussion of evidence or of characteristics. If you want to make personal friends with J, E, D and P, you must mark in colour in your own Bible what belongs to each,*—green for J with his vivid human stories, blue for E with his love of signs and wonders, brown for D the long-lost Law Book, and red for P, the lover of law and order. It does not take many hours to do, and once done, it is a treasure for life. But if you are the sort of person who 'hates patchwork Bibles,' consider this last sentence unread.

Enough has been said to show that the Pentateuch and the Former Prophets, which between them carry us from Creation to the Exile, were to a considerable extent 'written backwards'; that is to say, though they embody an older outlook in the Prophetic narrative, they view the earlier history with its admixture of myth and legend from the heights of their own times, and see its meaning primarily in the light of the great writing prophets from Amos onwards. And it is from that firm standpoint of

---

* Some of the passages are given in the Appendix; the complete list may be found in Driver's *Introduction to the Literature of the Old Testament*, or in Oesterley and Robinson's *Introduction to the Books of the Old Testament*.

indubitable history that we too shall get the true perspective of the Old Testament. For the Return and Restoration we have the books of Ezra and Nehemiah, based at any rate upon contemporary memoirs and the prophets Third-Isaiah,* Haggai, Zechariah and Malachi. After that there is no record of history in the Old Testament until the Books of Maccabees take it up in the second century; but external evidence is increasingly plentiful, and the religious development can be traced in the Psalms, the Wisdom literature, and the Book of Daniel, as well as in a number of extra-canonical works of the second and first centuries. The outward history and the inward development of revelation can thus be traced concurrently from Abraham to Christ.

A word is necessary in conclusion about the language of the Old Testament. Hebrew, being a Semitic language, is as different from an Aryan language such as English as it well can be. It is not merely that it is written from right to left, as originally was Greek, nor even that it has seven voices to its verbs; it differs in spirit as well as in structure. This may be exemplified in the one basic word, *Truth*. When the Greek talked about Truth he meant an intellectual abstraction which was the goal of human thought; but when the Hebrew spoke of Truth he meant *God acting*, and the root meaning of the word was *that-on-which-you-can-depend*. The language of the Chosen People is dominated by this central certainty of God which they alone possessed, and, as we shall see, their hope for the future was that God would still further reveal Himself in Self-consistent action. Nor were they disappointed of their hope, for when Pilate said: 'What is Truth?' in the Greek sense, the Truth Himself in the Hebrew sense was standing before him. So when Greek succeeded Hebrew as the language of revelation, the Hebrew word *'emeth,*† the adverbial form of which, *'amen,* passed into Greek as

* i.e. Is. lvi–lxvi.   † See further on p. 105.

the 'verily' of the gospels, had to be replaced by *aletheia*. Yet in the New Testament, as in the Old, 'Truth' still carries its Hebrew meaning, though the popular conception of it to-day is still largely Greek; whence come a good many misunderstandings.

To this difficulty of translation must be added the fact that until well on in the Christian era Hebrew was written with the consonants only, the vowels being supplied by the reader. In view of this the marvel is that the number of obscurities and variant readings is not vastly greater than it is. Our own language also has undergone three centuries of change since the appearance of the Authorised Version in 1611. The Old Testament is inevitably difficult; but to study the New Testament apart from it is like studying a plucked flower with no notion of the plant on which it grew; and to study the Bible at all in isolation from other branches of human knowledge, such as history and science, is like studying a plant apart from its soil and environment, and so to miss the cosmic significance of Christianity.

CHAPTER III

THE CREATION

To begin history with the Creation in these days provokes a smile, for it is the method of the fourth century rather than of the twentieth. Nevertheless Creation *was* the beginning of history, and for our purpose it is the reasonable starting point.

There are in the Book of Genesis two accounts of the Creation.* When Stephen Langton in the thirteenth century A.D., divided the Bible into chapters he made it vastly more convenient for reference, but his divisions were not based on Higher Criticism. Thus P's account of the Creation with which the book opens really ends in the middle of a verse with the words 'These are the generations of the heavens and of the earth when they were created.' If you put a full stop there and delete the 'and' at the beginning of the next verse, the second account, which belongs to J, begins: 'In the day that the Lord God made heaven and earth no plant of the field was yet in the earth,' and continues to the end of the chapter.

P's story, written during the Exile in Babylon, is a version of the Babylonian creation-myth, which the Chosen People either learned or relearned at that time. Now a myth is not a legend. A legend is a story which purports to be true as to facts, and consists actually of a kernel of history

* Note.—Scriptural references to each chapter will be found in the Appendix.

overlaid in the course of time with fanciful additions: such are the legends of our King Arthur. A myth is the attempt of primitive people to account in story-form for the facts of their experience,—for the existence of the world, as in the myth we are about to consider, for the succession of the seasons, as in the story of Demeter and Persephone, or for the feeling that man has somehow missed what he was intended for, as in the serpent story referred to on page 23. Thus myths are really primitive Theology. They do not necessarily record historical events, but they show how people tried to explain the facts of their experience in the dim ages of pre-history.

This Babylonian Creation story, as far as we know it, is as follows. All things were produced in the beginning from *Apsu*, the Ocean or Abyss, and *Tiamat* or Chaos, who is represented as a huge dragon. The gods, who came into being in a long succession, at length quarrelled with Tiamat; whereupon Merodach or Marduk, the sun-god, as champion of the gods attacked Tiamat and 'cleft her like a fish in two parts,' out of which he made respectively the earth and the firmament or heaven above it. Lastly he made the stars and the moon.

P also sees Creation as a victory of light over darkness; of Cosmos, which is Order, over Chaos; he recognises in it the same threefold division of ocean, earth, and firmament. Like the myth, he too puts the creation of the heavenly bodies *after* that of the earth; but there the resemblance ceases. Where the pagan sees Creation rising from a welter of warfare between rival and limited deities, the Jew sees it spring to being 'very good,' at the word of the One God. The opening words of Scripture, 'In the beginning *God*,' are the key to the whole. There is the truth, the certainty, that lies behind and beyond all history, the eternal, transcendent God, Who alone is utterly dependable. No one who reads both the pagan myth and the inspired can doubt their relationship; yet the difference between them is as that of light from darkness. In it we have another instance of the principle of Cana: the crude, polytheistic myth with just its kernel of truth cleansed and exalted into a medium of revelation.

We pass to J's story, which is three or four centuries older. Here both framework and atmosphere are different. J's story is even more unscientific than P's, for man appears on the scene first instead of last, but that is immaterial. Their business is to convey revelation, not to teach modern science. J's story adds something to P's, for in it, even more clearly than in P, the interest centres in man. Man is the head of Creation, to whom all lower creatures look as to their king, and man is the Lord God's friend.

The conception of God in J is as anthropomorphic as that in P is transcendent. The very word used for Creation is different. J's word means to form or to mould, as a potter moulds his clay, and he makes you feel that the Lord God planted the garden and put the man in it with His own Hands, tenderly and personally arranging every detail of his life; but P's word expresses Creation absolute, the Act peculiar to the Almighty, Who is far above all heavens and far removed from man. Yet these are but two sides of the same truth, for truth is always paradoxical, complete and satisfying just because it combines in perfect harmony apparent opposites which are both equally indispensable. We may thank God Who inspired him that R^{JP}, sitting with his sources before him twenty-four centuries ago, could not find it in his heart to leave out either story.

We have seen that these narratives convey three great truths: that God and God alone is the Author of Creation; that He created all things 'very good'; and that Man is at once the head of Creation, and made 'in God's Image' and capable of fellowship with Him.

Side by side with the record of revelation must be set the teaching of science.

Modern Science shows creation to be an organic unity. How matter itself came into being it cannot tell us; but it takes us back millions of years to a time when all the matter which constitutes the universe to-day existed in the form of a vast, nebulous mass of tenuous gas. This gas was made up of countless atoms of a relatively small number of elements, of which carbon, nitrogen, oxygen and hydrogen are among the commonest. The atom, though unthinkably small, is itself a composite structure, consisting of a central nucleus round which revolve electrons varying in number according to the element to which the atom belongs. These electrons are continually generating energy which, though it is constantly changing its form, can never be destroyed. It even seems probable that atoms can change into radiation, which if it be really so means that matter and light of every kind are but two different forms of energy. Every atom being thus a miniature powerhouse exerts a pull on others, and the stronger ones draw the weaker ones to themselves; so that by degrees condensations were formed in this tenuous gas, which were the beginnings of the stars and of our sun. This earth was once part of the sun, torn off it, probably by the attraction of a passing star, somewhere about two thousand million years ago, but still kept in perpetual motion round its parent by the latter's superior force of gravitation.

Thus the structure of a solar system is a replica on a vast scale of that of an atom.

The gaseous mass which was our earth in making gradually solidified, and owing to the peculiar composition of its atmosphere and its medium distance from the sun became, alone of all the heavenly bodies, apparently, capable of supporting life. . . . Life originated with a single cell,—

this also being built on the pattern of the atom with a central nucleus,—containing atoms of various elements *and* having the power of reproduction. From these unicellular organisms, which are estimated to have appeared first on this earth some three hundred million years ago, were evolved in slow stages and in gradual progression all the higher forms of life right up to man.

Between all the substances and organisms, which at any moment constitute creation, there goes on unceasing interchange of constituents and interaction of energy. But within the cosmic series every form of life has its own principle of unity, so that so long as it remains alive a tree goes on being a tree and an animal goes on being an animal both in spite and because of the constant stream of happening in which it is involved. Every form of created life, moreover, exists and reproduces with others of its kind; and each level of the series is not only progressively social and creative, but also shows an advance on the one below it in the direction of individuality. An individual means a single whole, and as even unicellular organisms are complex structures, it is clear that the universe is governed both in whole and part by this principle of unity in plurality. In regard to the development of the cosmic series, distinction of units is apparent even in those forms of life too low to be distinguished as either animal or vegetable; a little higher up the series, the difference between species is quite clear, but individual specimens still do not differ perceptibly. With the higher animals, however, each one differs from others of its kind in much more than mere appearance: a dog or an elephant, for instance, is even in a wild state much more individual than a frog or a fish. But it is only in man that this individuality becomes at last fully self-conscious and self-determining: the highest form of created individuality is human personality. With this there goes also a corresponding development on the

creative and social sides. In the higher animals the reproductive instinct operates with increasing consciousness and
deliberation, and finds further outlet in the making of
homes; and whether it be in the hive, the anthill, the herd,
or the smaller unit of the family, social life also develops.
But man and man alone is both capable of subordinating
his sexual desires to his will and of making, not homes
only but tools and pictures and words. He has an
awareness of himself, of his fellows and of the objects
around him beyond that of any lower animal; and he alone
has direct awareness of God. Man is the summit of the
cosmic series, but he shares its unfinished character. He
is not a terminus but a bridge; for, though the series is
summed up in him, he himself must reach out beyond
himself for satisfaction. It is a matter of universal experience that there is in man a sense of incompleteness
which cannot be satisfied within the series to which he
belongs. He can achieve completeness only through
self-transcendence.

At this point Science and Revelation meet. Genesis
says that man was made in the image of God: Science
shows that the cosmic series is built on a threefold principle;
individual, social and creative, which reaches a higher
stage of development in man than in any other
creature.

Now these three great principles, individual, social and
creative, which are progressively manifested in the cosmic
series and find their fullest expression in man *are the
constituents of love*. As a matter of experience, only persons
can love; and the power of loving develops in the series
concurrently with individuality, with which goes also the
power of self-determination, deciding for yourself what
you will or will not do.

Another name for this is free-will, which as we well
know is fully possessed by man alone; but a person cannot

love in isolation, for the essence of love is self-giving, and self-giving requires an object on which the gift may be bestowed. For its highest exercise it requires that its object should also be personal, because the purpose of its self-giving is that it may evoke response. A man may in a sense love a tree or a rock, because they have a certain individuality; but he knows very well that the tree and the rock cannot return his love. When a man loves a woman and elicits her love, both are richer for the giving, and when through the creative activity of sex their mutual love is embodied in a child, that child becomes a fresh object of the love of both his parents, and as his own personality develops he loves them in return. So the more love gives itself away the more there is of it. It is just as essentially creative and social as it is individual. So far Science and everyday experience; but Revelation goes further. It shows us that these three principles are manifested in creation *because they belong to the Being of God.* God Who is Unity in Plurality is Himself absolutely individual; He is social, comprising in His own Being a three-fold distinction of Person; and He is creative, ever giving Himself out, first and always in the depth of His own Being, and secondly in the material universe. This mutual Self-giving of the Trinity is Love; and creation is its projection in time and space.

Creation proceeds from Him, incorporates progressively His threefold likeness, becomes in man conscious of its dependence upon Him, and so moves towards Him as its true end. Man's first need, therefore, as well as his first duty, is worship, which is the creature's acknowledgement of dependence upon the Creator, and the response of love to love.

Thus in the marvel of the Divine Self-limitation, man, made in God's threefold Image, is His highest created means of expression; while in relation to the lower creation

he is at once its king and its priest, articulating its worship
to God, and mediating God to it.

Creation is the work of God Who is Trinity. Our
oldest Creed, worded before controversy rendered more
exact definition necessary, speaks of God the Father only
as 'Maker of Heaven and earth'; but the Nicene Creed,
while repeating this statement, adds that it is the Son,
called in the Fourth Gospel the Word, 'by Whom all
things were made,' and the Spirit Who is the Life-giver.
P knew nothing of distinction of Persons in God, but his
creation story adumbrates it, for God *said:* 'Let there be
light,' etc.; and the *Spirit* moved upon the face of the
waters. We shall see later on something of the way in
which these terms came into use; the point here is the
bearing of science on the Christian doctrine. Science,
though it cannot account for the origin of matter, does
show us quite clearly that its existence results in objects
and events. To take a concrete example: suppose that
a man is sitting under a tree with his dog, and that there
is a stone on the ground between them. Man, tree, dog,
and stone are all objects. The stone is the lowest kind of
object, because it is inanimate. Nevertheless it is a highly
complex entity consisting of a vast number of atoms
packed and held closely together by the energy within
them. Every one of those atoms is a theatre of intense
activity, generated by the unceasing movement of the
electrons. The activities within the stone are also con-
tinuously affected by and affecting those of the surrounding
atmosphere; and the stone itself is prevented from flying
off into space by the pull of the earth on which it lies.
The tree, though it belongs only to the subsidiary series
of vegetable life, is a highly complicated organism, of
course built of atoms, in which all sorts of movements and
processes are going on. Also and among other things, it is
intercepting the ray of light which in the last eight minutes
has travelled the ninety-six million miles from the sun to

earth, and so is throwing man, dog, and stone into shade. The dog's organism is involved in a still more complicated stream of unceasing event than the tree because, apart from his higher physical status, he is also directing a mental process beyond himself to the man, whom he wants to throw the stone for him. Lastly the man, in addition to the countless physiological and mental processes, conscious and unconscious, which constitute his being, is interacting with the eternal order, because he is wondering what will happen to him when he dies. At last he notices the dog and throws the stone. The dog barks, wags his tail, runs after the stone and brings it back; and man, dog, tree and stone are still themselves, though the stream of events in which they are involved has flowed on uninterruptedly. You may have watched them for ten minutes, and the scene of their activity has been a patch of ground twenty feet square. Yet physically the events in which these objects are concerned affect the whole universe, and mentally and spiritually their results are equally incalculable.

We might also remind ourselves that tree, dog, and man each started his individual life as a single cell, and the two latter in the course of a pre-natal period of nine weeks in the one case, and nine months in the other, re-capitulated all the stages of development through which the organic series passed as a whole before the evolution of their particular kind. We might reflect also that there is unbroken continuity of life in successive forms running back from each of those three organisms to the primeval single cell, so that each of them had ancestors of some sort living on earth at every moment of time since life first appeared. Again, the presence of the man in the group involves the presence of man-made objects, such as his clothes and his pipe. Animal, vegetable and mineral have all contributed to these, but they were all made out of existing material and obey the universal laws of matter. The whole group man, dog, tree, stone, earth, air, sun, clothes, pipe are all built of atoms which in a constant succession of forms and stream of happening have been in the universe *since the beginning*. And there Revelation steps in with, 'In the beginning *GOD* . . . '; and while attributing to the First Person of the Trinity the Will whence all proceeds, ascribes to the Second and Third functions which correspond very closely to the two forms of creative activity manifested respectively in objects and events. The Father is the Fountain-head and the Source of all volition, Who makes matter to be; the Son is the Creative Word, Who makes things to be things, and to continue in being through the passage of circumstance; the Spirit is the Breath of ever-moving life and the motive power of events.

Before we leave the subject of creation, there is one other point to notice in connection with man. Though on his first emergence he was truly the crown of the created order and the highest created incorporation of the Divine Likeness, he was then in a state only of *potential* perfection. Just as one may hold in one's hand a sound acorn and say truly, 'This is a potential oak tree,' so man as created was potentially perfect man, but with all his development before him. The 'very good'-ness of creation which culminated in him had yet to be actualised, and could be so actualised only by man's reaching out beyond himself to God Whose Likeness he was. Picture then the first human pair as God made them, in whom potentially was all the human race, set in the earth so wonderfully prepared for them, with all their future before them. What ought to have followed? If you could plant an acorn to-day, and then go out every day for a hundred years or so to look at it, the difference from day to day would be imperceptible, but at the end of the time there would be a forest tree; and there is a great deal of difference between a forest tree and the acorn from which it grew, though the tree existed potentially in the acorn from the first.

By some such gradual process the human race ought to have gone steadily forward to its goal.

It did not do so.

To take another illustration.   Man, as created, was like one who stands at the foot of a mountain, with a straight steep track leading before him to the summit.   All he had to do was to climb.

Why did he not do so?

CHAPTER IV

THE FALL

THE story of the Fall of Man in the third chapter of Genesis belongs to J, and follows directly on his account of the Creation. Here again the transmuting principle is at work, for the story is based on an ancient Babylonian myth framed to account for human mortality, which the Hebrews probably brought with them from their Mesopotamian home.

According to this myth there was in the 'fields of the blessed' a tree whose fruit conveyed immunity from death; it was intended for man, but the serpent, always regarded by the ancients as uncannily wise, got it first, and so cheated man of his birthright. There are here two elements of truth; that man was meant to be immortal, and that immortality in some way comes through eating. The story is, however, completely non-moral; man's bondage to death is not his fault, but merely a piece of bad luck.

J, on the other hand, makes the serpent the enemy of God, who competes with Him for man's allegiance. Man, who appears as possessing both spiritual understanding and a moral nature, by his own choice forfeits the blessing intended for him, and is punished accordingly. Yet even as the doom falls, there is given a hope of recovery; for the seed of the woman shall bruise the serpent's head.

This story has been described as a drama in three scenes. In the first scene the actors are God and Man; in the second they are God, Man, and the serpent; in the third God, Man, the serpent, and the serpent's conqueror.

There are several things to notice before examining the teaching which gathers round this story.

23

In the first place, we do not believe in the Fall of Man because of the story of Adam and Eve, any more than we believe in rainbows because of the story of the Flood. We believe in the Fall because, though sin is universal in human experience, so also is the sense that it ought not to be. We each of us have the witness in ourselves that the human race has somehow taken a wrong turning. This universal consciousness is expressed in the Adam story but is not derived from it. The Adam story has therefore been aptly compared to the pillared front of a great modern building, which is, however, actually upheld, not by the columns of the façade, but by an unseen framework of steel.

In the second place we muŝt note that this story as it stands makes no attempt to account for the *ultimate* origin of evil, nor does it even explicitly identify the serpent with him whom after ages called Satan or the Adversary: it merely recounts the first human sin. Neither is that sin specifically connected with the subsequent sinfulness of humanity; in fact, J's theory about that is given elsewhere in the story of the angel marriages, 'the only piece of unrevised mythology in the Old Testament.'

In view of these facts it will be worth while to trace the history of the Adam story and the problems which it raises. The Chosen People had learnt before the time of J that sin is *moral* evil, the root of which is disobedience; and this the story clearly conveys. It was the shock of the Exile which brought them to a new realisation of the sinfulness of sin, and so led them to wrestle with the problem of its origin. To this problem their captors in Babylon already had an answer in the dualism native to the East, which holds that there are two eternal Sources, one of good, and one of evil, locked in unending conflict. This doctrine, hopeless since it promises no end to evil, the monotheistic Jew could not accept; he stood to it that there was but One God, but could at first see no other course open to him than to attribute to the One God the origin of both good and evil, a view actually expressed by the Second-Isaiah. This solution, however, could not satisfy those who had been nourished on First-Isaiah's doctrine of the Divine Holiness. They felt that somehow or other the responsibility for human sin must rest with man, not with his Creator. Thus it was that R^{JP} in the fourth century put J's story of the primal disobedience into the forefront of the Pentateuch; and some two hundred years later the author of the Book of Jubilees went a step further, and traced all human sinfulness to the infection of the first.

This theory of the origin of human evil did not at once find universal acceptance. Both up to and during the time of Our Lord, it was held concurrently with two others, —that already referred to of the angel marriages; and another, based on a phrase in the same passage, of the 'evil imagination,' which according to the Rabbis was implanted in every individual at birth. Of both these views there are traces in the New Testament. Our Lord Himself, dealing with sin and its author as He found them, made no recorded pronouncement as to its origin; and it was left to St. Paul, by his use of the Adam story to demonstrate Christ as the Second Adam, to exalt it to the unique position which it has ever since occupied.

Thus does the Holy Spirit guide the questing minds of men step by step into all truth.

So far as its doctrinal import is concerned, the story of Adam and Eve may be taken either literally or allegorically, and has been so taken at least from the second century A.D. Modern thinkers in choosing the allegorical view have but reverted to a method of interpretation at least as old as the literalism of the Reformation. Actually the bulk of scientific opinion at the present favours belief in the origin of the human race from a single pair, and thus far concurs with Genesis; but the truths conveyed by the inspired story are the same, whichever way it is interpreted.

The teaching derived from and connected with the Adam story may now be summarised.

It is evident that the sin of man was not the beginning of evil. The first sentence of the story raises a problem which it does not attempt to solve. God has an enemy; personal evil walks in His world; how did it get there? There is no one inclusive scriptural pronouncement on this subject; but the consensus of Jewish and Christian opinion is that the original or ultimate Fall consisted in the voluntary rebellion of created and finite wills against God before the appearance of man on this planet. The authors of this pre-human revolt were spiritual beings commonly called angels, and their leader was Lucifer, or Light-bearer, who by his sin became Satan, the Adversary, and Prince of Darkness. With regard to this fall of the angels it has been conjectured that the cause of their rebellion was jealousy of the honour to be bestowed upon the human race,—the younger creation, in the Incarnation; and also that, being purely spiritual beings, they foresaw as man could not do, the consequences of disobedience, and so, sinning with their eyes open, were self-inhibited from repentance. It is suggested also that Lucifer before his Fall had this earth in his charge and consequently tried to implicate it in his revolt. On this last hypothesis it is possible that the life-force of the universe was somehow vitiated by the fall of Lucifer at the outset of its development; and if this be so, the evolution of evil forms of life, such as disease bacilli, may be the result of that vitiation. This view in no way implies that God forsook His creation, but rather that He continued to guide and sustain the impaired life-force within it in accordance with His original purpose.

The recognition of the undoubted fact that the fall of man was not the ultimate origin of evil, combined with

what has already been said about the undeveloped nature
of human perfection, puts the Fall story in a rather different
light from that in which most of us were brought up to
regard it. The first human sin appears no longer as a
fall from a great height to a corresponding depth, but
rather as a transgression, a stepping aside from the straight
path of progress up the mountain on to a side-track that
proved to be a *cul-de-sac*. Nevertheless it is clear that
man was free. Whatever antecedent infection of evil there
may have been in the universe, he was not obliged to
sin; and the consequences of his transgression were no
less disastrous for being unforeseen.

The whole subject of the origin and nature of evil is
deeply mysterious; but two things are clear. Evil had
a beginning; and God did not make it. Lucifer, as he
left the creative Hand of God was as lovely as Gabriel
or Michael. God made him an angel; he made himself
a devil. Moreover just as Genesis proclaims that evil
had a beginning, so does the Apocalypse almost shout
at us that it will have an end. Between that beginning
and that end lies the long process of Restoration; the
method of which is that the evil itself shall be made
instrumental to good.

It remains to consider the nature of Adam's temptation,
and the consequences of his sin.

The attack of the Tempter was launched against faith
and love and obedience, which are the constituents of
man's response to God. First he suggested doubt of the
loving wisdom of God's enactments: 'Yea, *hath* God
said . . .?' and then that good rather than evil would result
from disobedience. This sin of our first parents so
damaged their nature that neither they nor those whom
they begat could realise the perfection for which they were
intended. In some mysterious way it also affected the
whole lower creation, of which man is the head, so that
the *whole* creation was withheld from its movement towards

God. The possibility already suggested of a still earlier infection of the universe with evil in no way precludes this further implication of it in the Fall of Man, which is conveyed in the Genesis story by the words: 'Cursed be the ground for thy sake; thorns and thistles shall it bring forth to thee.' Our knowledge of the solidarity of the universe from the scientific as well as from the theological standpoint makes such an implication not only intelligible but inevitable. Thus at the outset man failed in his duty to the lower creation, whose king and priest he was. By his transgression it, too, in some mysterious way was turned aside from the straight path of progress. But that which was included in man's fall was from the first also included in his restoration; and when at last the Second Adam mounted the Cross, 'not for our sins only but for the sins of the whole universe,' the kingly crown that graced His priestly act was made of *thorns*.

The root of the injury was in the *will* of man. His nature as created was so delicately balanced that the faculties, including free-will, which distinguished him from the lower animals, outweighed the part of his nature which he shares with them, and so raised him above the necessity of physical death which lies upon all other life; but when once the will in response to the Tempter's suggestion had acted in disobedience to God, it lost its sovereignty over the other faculties, and the balance of human nature was destroyed. Thereafter man's life-story ceased to resemble that of the acorn, which progresses imperceptibly to perfection. Henceforth, as the caterpillar turns into the chrysalis, his path must lead to the great change of death, beyond which, apart from the intervention of God, he is powerless to proceed. The inherited weakness of will in human nature which results from the Transgression is commonly called Original Sin. The word 'original' means 'coming from the source or fountain-head,' and cannot be improved upon; but 'Sin' in this context is misleading, because it implies responsibility, and it is not possible that a just and loving God should hold us personally responsible for the sin of our first parents.

The doctrine of Original Sin is really an outgrowth of the practice of Infant Baptism. Since the Church did as a matter of fact baptise Infants, and the Creed said that there was but 'one Baptism for the remission of sins' it was argued that there must be in the infant some sin to remit, though evidently it was of a different nature from the actual sin of older and responsible persons. Much controversy has centred round this point; but the fact that emerges is that there is in us all, in consequence of our membership in the human race, an inherited weakness of the faculty of free-will, which, like the bias in bowls that makes them roll them out of the straight, predisposes us to actual sin.

Incidentally, modern psychology teaches exactly the same thing in different words. It tells us that we have three primary instincts, each issuing in a corresponding complex, which lies just below the level of consciousness. There is the instinct of the Ego or Self, which is concerned with the individual's own maintenance and development; in this the will is rooted. There is the instinct of Sex, which though concerned primarily with the reproduction of our kind, finds further creative outlet in the arts of civilisation; and there is the Herd instinct, in which is rooted the moral sense which is concerned with the relations of the individual to society. Experience shows the Herd instinct to be universally weaker than the other two. Human nature still bears the threefold seal of the Divine Likeness; but it has lost its balance and its unity, both as a whole and in each of its parts. The individual is ever at tension with society, and society is marred by selfishness and sensuality. The Fall is rightly called the Counter-Creation for the result of the dethronement of the will, in the individual as in the world at large, is Chaos in the place of Cosmos.

There is however another side.   As with a stream rising
in the hills that is subsequently polluted by contact with
a lead-mine, so the source of our life remains pure.   The
poison does not flow upstream; behind the original guilt
there is the still more original innocence.   Free-will also,
though impaired, is still ours.   God's loving purpose still
holds and the Restoration is even now in progress.   Every
butterfly that emerges is a pledge that in spite of the Fall
and our ensuing bondage to death 'it doth not yet appear
what we shall be.'

CHAPTER V

FROM THE FALL TO THE CALL OF ABRAHAM

THE eight chapters of Genesis following on the Fall story are made up of alternate portions of J and P. J's interest continues to centre in humanity. First he gives the story of Cain and Abel and the origin of the arts; then that of the angel marriages and the shortening of the span of human life in order the sooner to work out the evil introduced by them. This he follows rather inconsequently by the story of the Flood, a second remedy for the same evil, since by it all the wicked were eliminated and the race reduced to a faithful remnant of eight. Finally he gives the story of the confusion of tongues at Babel, a myth indeed, but one of profound significance, for it shows the fallen race trying to live in independence of God and at strife within itself. The name Babel, which probably means confusion, reappears in Babylon, the scene of the Exile of the Chosen People, and the symbol in apocalyptic language of the sinful world.

P contributes the generations of man from Adam to Shem, and from Shem to Abraham, and a variant version of the Flood story, which the redactor has combined with J's.* The section as a whole accounts quite satisfactorily

---

* There are Flood legends almost all the world over. The Mesopotamian flood is corroborated both by cuneiform inscriptions from Nineveh, dating from before 2,000 B.C. and by the discovery at Ur of eight feet of unstratified alluvial deposit between the remains of neolithic occupation and those of later civilisation. Its date is given tentatively as between 4,250 and 4,200 B.C.

from the standpoint of its own age for the origins of human civilisation, and finally links those origins with Abraham. We who know something of the antiquity of man may smile, for Abraham lived only about four thousand years ago, and it is probable that man has walked the earth for some three hundred thousand, compared with which the nineteen generations into which P so tidily condenses pre-history are as a drop in a bucket. Yet we have nothing very definite to put in their place, though it is certain that as the human race increased in numbers and improved in physique and mentality, gradually, by slow stages, the great racial types were evolved, each with its own group of languages, and that which we call civilisation made its appearance. Now man's first business is to live; and it is only when living becomes comparatively easy that he has leisure for the arts. Consequently the earliest civilisations were located in great river valleys, where food was easy to come by, the climate equable and the land capable of supporting a considerable population. The so-called 'dawn of history' thus occurred more or less simultaneously in Mesopotamia, the land-between-the-rivers Tigris and Euphrates, and in the Nile valley of Egypt. Between these two and bordering on the Great Sea lay the little land of Canaan, the stage set ready for the drama of Redemption. The spade of the archaeologist has brought to light many features of these ancient civilisations, including some evidence as to their religion, which shows as clearly as does Genesis the fallenness of the race. Some years ago, moreover, a practically certain identification was established between two Mesopotamian kings named in inscriptions and two mentioned in Genesis as contemporaries of Abraham; Hammurabi* being Amraphel, King of Shinar, and Kudur-lagamur Chedorlaomer of Elam. As

---

* Hammurabi was the sixth of the dynasty of Amorite kings, who ruled the Plain of Shinar from about 2050–1750 B.C. and made Babylon its capital.

these are computed to have lived about twenty centuries before Christ, we have a fairly definite starting point
for the history of the Chosen People.

History recovered from cuneiform inscriptions helps us
to a background as well as a date. It seems that the Land
between the Rivers consisted at this time of a number of
little states, subject to frequent incursions of their powerful
neighbours from Elam, under the dynasty of the aforesaid
Kudur-lagamur. It was probably in order to escape
massacre that Terah the Semite with all his family left his
home at Ur near the Persian Gulf and made for the north-
west.* Having got as far as Haran in the Upper Euphrates
Terah died, leaving his son Abraham as head of the caravan, and in a strange land.

Then something happened.

All through the countless ages since the Fall the work of
Restoration had been going on, as it were underground.
We cannot trace its progress. At this point it comes up
to the surface; the hidden process culminates in an historic
event. The first great crisis in the period of preparation
is reached and passed. As Genesis shows, all previous
history led up to Abraham.

It seems about as certain as anything can be that the
Semitic conception of God was henotheistic; that is to say,
the Semites believed that each district had its own god,
called by the nomads the *'El* or *'Elōhîm*, which means the
Strong One† and by the agricultural tribes the *Ba'al*,
which means Owner or Husband.

The tribal god was regarded as a friendly being, linked
to his worshippers by a bond of kinship, but bound

* Shortly after Terah's migration Hammurabi repelled the Elamites,
and united all the little states into one great Empire.

† *'Elōhîm* is the plural of *'El*, but it is often used interchangeably
with it to denote one God, the plural here conveying the idea not of
many-ness but of majesty.

D

primarily to his land. Since on this view to leave your country was to leave your God, Abram, already childless, was bereft of his deity and of his father at one stroke.

The moment of his extremity was the opportunity for which God waited. Abram in his need reached out beyond himself for help; and God answered with revelation, 'the creative activity of God drawing man to his true end.' In a profound spiritual experience, the manner of which is not told us, he apprehended the fact that his God had come with him from Chaldaea, and was there with him in Haran, calling him on yet further into an unknown land.

Conditional on his obedience was a threefold promise. His seed, though he was as yet without issue, should possess that land; they should become a great nation; and in them all the families of the earth should be blessed.

*So Abram went.**

Thus briefly does Scripture record this crisis in the world's history. It is a sentence which, together with two others, might well be printed in letters of gold. When Abraham turned his obedient steps towards the land of promise, he did that which entitled him to be known to all ages as the father of the faithful, for that act of obedience was also a sublime act of faith, rooted in the conception of deity which was to be the treasure of his seed, namely that *God is true.* Mere henotheist as he was, Abraham's creed was 'I believe *in* God,' and his steadfastness in it puts us monotheists to shame. He did not merely believe that God was real, but that He was dependable Reality. God had made promises conditional on obedience: if the obedience did not fail neither would the promises. God is utterly reliable, and obedience always brings a blessing,— that is the starting-point of revealed religion.

* Abram is the earlier form of his name. According to P it was changed to Abraham, which means 'father of a great multitude' to remind him of the promise.

By this act of faith and his subsequent persistence in it Abraham became the first stone of the bridge which was to span the gulf between God and fallen man.

Twenty-one centuries were to pass in the building of it: stone by stone it must grow on either side, the Action of God invoking the response of man, until there should lack only the Keystone to complete the arch.

First the foundation-stone destined to uphold so weighty a structure must himself be tested, not only by the long delay in the advent of the promised son, but also by the command to offer in sacrifice him upon whom all the promises depended. Before either the first or the second promise could be fulfilled Abraham's seed must leave the land they had not yet possessed, sojourn for four hundred years in Egypt, and return to it by way of forty years in the wilderness that should make them at last a nation. They must occupy and settle the Promised Land under Joshua, hold it precariously under the Judges, rise under the monarchy at last to prominence among the nations, only to lose their national unity in the Divided Kingdom.

Two centuries later the ten northern tribes must be conquered by and absorbed into Assyria, leaving the hope of the future focussed on Judah under the Davidic kings. Then Judah also must be led captive, not to Assyria but to Babylonia, whence Abraham had come sixteen centuries before, where the Chosen People must be melted down in the furnace of affliction, in order that with the advent of Cyrus a purged remnant may return to refound their nationhood, though not their independence, at Jerusalem. When the Persian Empire falls before the great Alexander, they must once more change their masters; and through the peril and the enlargement of Greek influence, the saving fires of persecution and a brief period of virtual independence, pass at length beneath the yoke of Rome. Then, in the days of the first Augustus, the third promise should be fulfilled, and in the seed of Abraham all the families of the earth be blessed.

Abraham, with his back to the great rivers and his face to Canaan, knew nothing of all that. He simply *believed in* God.

CHAPTER VI

THE CHOSEN PEOPLE

(i) From Abraham to Moses

Our next task is to follow the course of history outlined at the close of the last chapter, and with it the development of the revelation which culminated in the Incarnation.

We have seen that Abraham inherited from his fathers a relatively pure though strictly limited conception of God, which advanced in his own person through his apprehension of the facts that God was bound to himself rather than to his country, and that He was utterly to be trusted.

We have yet to see how, among Abraham's seed, his primitive creed of 'I believe in God' developed into belief in one only God, and Him holy; and how that in its turn was the foundation of the revelation of the Trinity.

Of the four or five centuries during which Abraham and his immediate descendants lived in but did not possess the land of Canaan, our earliest records are the narratives of J and E, written from eight to twelve centuries after the events which they relate, but embodying much older material. The still later P is valueless as an authority on origins, but for these we are fortunately not solely dependent upon Genesis. Much of undoubtedly primitive custom may be gathered from other parts of the Prophetic narrative, and from sources both within and without the Bible we have some knowledge of Semitic religion as a whole. For it must never be forgotten that the seed of revelation was first sown in the soil of natural religion, and that that soil was divinely prepared. God did not leave the world to the mercy of the devil and its own devices for countless ages, and then suddenly in the twenty-first century B.C. begin to do something. The world has all along been wrapped round in His Love, though the unveiling of His plan for Redemption began only with Abraham; and as with our bodies, so with our religion, it is first that which is natural, then that which is spiritual. So we, who inherit something of the Jew's sense of superiority over those outside the Covenant, must face the fact that until four thousand years ago all the people in the world were heathen, and that God, Who had been ceaselessly at work among them from the beginning, then took a very good heathen and began to teach him. This process illustrates both the mystery of the swaddling bands, God limiting Himself with imperfect instruments, and through them achieving His purpose none the less, and the mystery of Cana, the transmutation of things poor and limited into infinite riches. What, then, was the religion of the Patriarchs? Religion is always to some extent related to character, and character is influenced by environment. The Semites were a pastoral people, and if your chief interest in life is sheep, you must live in places where there are few people and much pasture; go with your flocks to the feeding grounds, and sleep or wake with them under the stars. Abraham's migration to Canaan was of twofold importance to his seed. It removed them from the polytheistic atmosphere of the Mesopotamian cities, and it ensured that for some centuries they should continue to be shepherds, who are of all men most wakeful to the Voice of God. Consequently the chief characteristic of the Patriarchs was spiritual alertness. Their lives were punctuated and ruled by contacts with God; and following an instinct by no means peculiar to the Semites they accounted the scene of a theophany or manifestation of the deity as a holy place,—a *Bethel* or House of God.

It often happened that a natural object such as a tree or a stone was involved in the spiritual experience; and where this was so the object came to be regarded as related to the God rather as body is to soul, and was venerated accordingly. If the natural object was lacking, an artificial one, a pillar of stone or wood, might be substituted. We do not know when this practice originated, but the pillars formed a regular part of the furnishing of a holy place after the return to Canaan and until much later times.* It is probable that idols originated from an attempt to carve these pillars into some sort of form. There is no trace of this among the Patriarchs, but until we know for certain what the teraphim and the ephod were, we cannot tell whether or no images played any part in their religion.

It seems clear that the presence of the deity at the holy place was acknowledged in two ways: first by a humble access expressed in ablutions and removal of the shoes; secondly by some form of sacrifice.

Sacrifice is as obscure in its origin as it is varied in its form. We do not know who offered the first sacrifice, or what he meant by it; but this much is certain; the root idea which underlies sacrifice all the world over is *Fellowship*.

Sacrifice therefore exists primarily and essentially in God Who, Himself both Individual and Social, is ever giving and taking in the depths of His Own Being; and Creation was a further act of Sacrifice on His part because it was, and its continued being *is* a further giving out of Himself. That Divine Self-giving is to be answered on behalf of the whole creation by the conscious, willing self-giving of man, who, made in His Maker's threefold image, can find no satisfaction save in fellowship with Him.

Ultimately and ideally, then, sacrifice is the same as love, and it certainly has no essential connection with

* In our Bible the word 'pillar' is chiefly used for the *Massebāh* or obelisk; while the *'Ashērāh* or wooden pillar is left untranslated.

Sacrifice is
love & has no
connection with

either suffering or sin. The fact that it is universally
practised by man shows that, though fallen, he still retains
his God-likeness, and cannot be happy out of his right
relationship with Him. The presence of evil in the world,
by putting an obstacle in the way of this mutual self-giving
between God and man, has introduced into sacrifice the
element of suffering. Consequently, just so far as man
has any sense of alienation from his God, to that extent
also there enters into his practice of sacrifice the idea of
propitiation. This however does not necessarily spring
from any sense of *sin*. The Hebrew word for propitiate
or reconcile really means to wipe clean; and in its primitive
usage probably refers more to the clearing of the Divine
Face, blackened by anger, than to the cleansing of human
guilt. The idea of the deity as capricious is common in
natural religion; but though misfortune was attributed to
His whim more readily than to His people's guilt, He had
none the less to be propitiated. It was just these non-
moral ideas of God and consequently of propitiation,
which the Hebrew conception of His truth and holiness
was designed to correct; but just how far along this path
the Patriarchs had progressed we have no knowledge.

Since man is so constituted that he cannot express
himself otherwise than through his body and other material
means, sacrifice involves for him the use of a physical
medium: a material gift must express his intention, and,
if possible effect his desire. It is evident that in the time
of the Patriarchs at least two types of sacrifice were in use.
The first, the libation of oil or other liquid, required no
other furniture than the sacred stone or pillar at the Bethel.
For the other, animal sacrifice offered by fire, there was
required also 'the place of slaughter' or altar, built of
earth or unhewn stones.

Since fire cannot safely be kindled near dwellings or
crops, these sacrifices were offered on bare hill-tops,—
witness Isaac's on Mount Moriah,—sanctuaries which

reappear in later history as in the 'high places,' furnished with altar, obelisk and pillar.

The thought of animal sacrifice is distasteful to modern minds and we tend to regard it as merely barbarous and revolting. Men of an earlier age, however, less refined in their physical senses than we, but possibly more discerning of fundamentals, were filled with awe at the sight of shed blood because as a matter of experience, *the life was in it.*

It was—and is, extremely mysterious; but to them its mystery, like that of other things, was not absolute but relative: it was good or bad according to the circumstances of the percipient. If you killed your brother in anger it was bad; if he was killed as a sacrifice to God, it was good, the very best gift that could be offered. That is why the Latin word *sacer* carries the double meaning of sacred and accursed.

The example given above makes plain the fact that the sacrificial value of a death depended upon the intention with which the victim was killed. A sacrificial killing was not done with the intention of destroying life, but with the intention both of releasing the life to go as a gift to God, and of promoting life in those who offered the sacrifice. This intention of sacrifice was expressed in certain ritual acts: these and these alone invested the death with sacrificial significance. The blood of the victim was sprinkled on the worshippers. Part of its body,—in some cases the whole,—was consumed by fire, which signified both the etherealisation of that portion for God's use, and His acceptance of the whole. Where a portion only was so consumed the rest of the victim's body remained as food for the worshippers. As far back as we have any knowledge, animal sacrifice was followed on most occasions by this sacrificial meal: the flesh of the victim, having been given to God by man and by Him accepted and given back to them, was regarded as in some sense His own flesh, the vehicle of His life, and so the effective instrument of fellowship between them.

The occasions upon which sacrifice was offered appear to have been of two kinds,—the extraordinary and the ordinary. In the earlier narratives a theophany is acknowledged by the recipient on the spot by some form of sacrifice. The story of Isaac shows plainly that human sacrifice was an accepted part of Abraham's religion, a fact amply corroborated by recent excavations at Ur, while the story of Jephthah's daughter in the period of the Judges shows that the practice had at least survived the sojourn in Egypt. There is evidence also that it was resorted to in degenerate times as late as the seventh century. Of ordinary occasions there seem to have been few, but such as there were arose from the life of the people. There was certainly a feast when the firstlings of the flock were offered, and probably another at sheep-shearing; possibly one or two others connected with the moon and the stars, which mean so much to watchful shepherds. All these were occasions of great social festivity as well as of worship; and the sacrifices were essentially tribal acts, in which the normal officiant was the head of the clan, for kingship and priesthood always go together with primitive peoples. The Patriarch offered the sacrifice, not as possessing that which others had not, but as their representative.

Thus far we have considered only the manner and occasions of Semitic worship; it remains to see in what way the worship ruled the life. Here again it is hard to come by quite certain knowledge. The institution of the Sabbath is probably very ancient; that of Circumcision, though practised by many Semitic tribes and attributed by P to Abraham, appears not to have been a distinguishing mark of the Chosen People until the Exile. A food law there certainly was: certain animals were unclean and therefore forbidden as food; and no meat might be eaten with the blood in it. Now why? Again the mystery, so familiar and so unfathomable,—*because the life is in the blood*.

There, then, is the starting-point. It is all very groping and inchoate, much of it negative and non-moral, much mixed with evil; but as a teacher builds carefully on what his pupils already know, so God took all this crude outgrowth of human consciousness, and broad-based upon it the revelation of Himself. It is through these primitive ideas of sacrifice, purified and enlarged through succeeding centuries, that we are able to understand something of what happened on Calvary; and the Slain yet Living Lamb Who is the centre of the civilisation of Heaven derives His title as well as His humanity from pastoral Abraham.

The earliest chapter in the history of Abraham's seed closed with their migration to Egypt, which is variously dated from the seventeenth to the fifteenth century B.C.* The circumstances which led to it are told conjointly by J and E, in a cycle of stories of which Joseph is the hero.

It is probable that this settlement in Egypt was intended only for the duration of the famine. No move, however, was made in that generation; and before long a change of dynasty on the Egyptian throne made return impossible. The descendants of those who had come as honoured guests were forced to remain as slaves. There is great difference of opinion as to the length of the sojourn in Egypt, but it was at any rate long enough to allow many generations to grow up to whom Canaan was but a name, and the promises to Abraham a dim tradition. It is strange that J and E, who have such vivid narratives of the Patriarchal Period, have preserved nothing of this except its happy beginning and its dramatic close; stranger still that in after times the Chosen People should show scarcely any trace of Egyptian influence.

All through these dark centuries they kept their tribal

* For the probability that *not all* the tribes migrated, see footnote, p. 51.

identity and customs, language and traditions; and in spite of oppression increased mightily in numbers. At the same time no people can live for centuries in bondage and fail to acquire something of the serf mentality. Those who are always oppressed and on the defensive become weak-spirited and lacking in initiative. Yet though Israel in Egypt was inferior in morale to the free tribe which Israel himself had brought down, they were powerful enough to make the reigning Pharaoh wish to get rid of them. The order for the destruction of the boy babies was a policy of extermination; if there were no males in the next generation and the women married Egyptians, the tribe would cease to exist.

At that juncture came Moses, Egyptian bred but Hebrew born, and wholly Hebrew at heart. His court upbringing gave him the power of leadership, the influence of his mother Jochebed ensured his faithfulness to his race.

There are really three accounts of the call of Moses, those of J and E woven together, and another by P, which adds little to it. The essential facts are clear. Moses killed an Egyptian who was ill-treating a Hebrew. Then, hot with resentment against the oppressors of his people, he fled to the wilderness of Sinai and settled there. One day, when this palace-bred Hebrew was keeping sheep like his ancestors, he had a theophany, which E connects with the burning bush. Once again the Action of God called for human faith and obedience under circumstances which rendered their successful issue contrary to all human probability. Moses was to deliver the Hebrews from Egypt and to take them back to Canaan.

In this theophany to Moses a new content was given to the Divine Name of Jahveh. The previous history of this name is obscure, for though J uses it from the beginning it certainly was not generally used until this time. Its derivation is equally uncertain: it may have come from a verb meaning *to blow*, and so mean the storm-god; or it may be connected with the same verb in the causative sense of overthrow, and so mean the destroyer or lightning-god, like the Saxon Thor; but on this occasion it was definitely connected with the verb *to be*. Moses was told to tell the Hebrews that *I will be* had sent him.* *I will be* in Hebrew is Ehjeh, and Jahveh is the same in the third person. So the God of Israel from His home in Sinai declares Himself to be in relation to His people *He Who will be*. He is the God Who throughout their history will be always revealing Himself in Self-consistent Action. The title is apt in its very vagueness, for there could be no summing up of all that was to come. Nevertheless the Hebrews were to have proof soon enough that Jahveh was a God of Action.

Through the mists of time and the intricacy of the threefold narrative the main events of the Great Deliverance are clear. The plagues which followed the Pharaoh's refusal to liberate the Hebrews culminated in the slaying of the firstborn. Of the households of Egypt the Hebrews alone, who had that night offered their ancient sacrifice of the firstlings of the flock, had not one dead. Thus the old feast was charged with new meaning and became the Passover, for in the language of later times the destroying angel had then passed over their houses because he saw on their door-posts the blood of the slain lamb. The next day they started for Canaan by way of the wilderness.

We were brought up to believe that the water which stretched before the Israelites when the Egyptians were found to be pursuing was the western arm of the Red Sea, which came some distance further inland then than now. Actually, as the location of the sites of this journey dates only from the first century A.D. it is quite likely that

---

* See R. V. margin. The alternative translation 'I am' expresses what God is in His own eternal, timeless Being. 'I will be' expresses His relation to His people, in which that Being is progressively revealed. The one is the complement of the other.

this supposition is wrong, and that the route taken to avoid the coast *road* was *the coast itself* where for thirty miles a narrow strip of sand separates the Mediterranean from the shallow and normally dry basin of Lake Bardawil, to the south of which lies the road.* In that case it is probable that the Egyptians tried to intercept the Israelites by cutting across the dry bed of the lake and, as J's account suggests, were bogged. Then the sea, as is its wont under a strong wind, breached the sandy spit *behind* the fleeing Israelites and flooded the lake with the Egyptians in it. Where and how the thing happened is, however, secondary. The important thing is that the sea so moved at that moment as to drown the pursuing host and let the seed of Abraham, with the sea on either hand, go free. God had acted. He had shown Himself to be true as Abraham had believed Him. He was Jahveh, God of the Hebrews, and He was incomparably strong.

The prophetic narrative of the wilderness period runs intermittently through Exodus and Numbers, and is resumed and concluded at the very end of Deuteronomy. On the first stage of the journey occurred the giving of the manna and the water from the rock, provisions for their bodily needs which plainly showed the continuance of Jahveh's care. Equally plain in the story is the temper of the tribes whom the next forty years were to hammer into a nation. Even from such signal wonders as those of the Exodus and the wilderness, this people stultified by bondage was slow to draw confidence for the future. No matter how great the last obstacle surmounted, they could never see over the next fence. Faith in God, such as

---

* This view is supported by the fact that the Hebrew *Yam Suf*, translated Red Sea, means really Sea of Reeds, a description which applies perfectly to Lake Bardawil but not at all to the Gulf of Suez. Yet another theory makes Sinai a volcano east of the Gulf of Akaba, and accounts for the parting of the waters and the pillar of cloud and fire by a seismic disturbance such as accompanied the eruption of Mont Pelé in 1902.

Abraham had, was at this time mostly left to their leader.

The central point of the wilderness wanderings was the encampment before the mountain which J calls Sinai and E Horeb, 'the mount of God' and of the Covenant. Tradition identifies this with the so-called Mount Moses in the extreme south of the peninsula; but on the view that the Israelites took the coast route a more likely site is provided by Gebel Hellal or Mount Lawful in the north-east, which, though less impressive than Mount Moses, rises a sheer two thousand feet above an alluvial plain far more capable of supporting a large caravan than the barren wilderness of the south. Here again, however, it is not the place that matters but what happened there.

Leaving the tribes encamped at the foot of the mountain Moses went up to receive for them a revelation; and returned with what we call the Ten Commandments. He told these to the tribes and they replied, 'All the words that Jahveh hath spoken we will do.' A single altar and a stone pillar for each tribe were then erected, and sacrifices offered; Moses read the Ten Words again, receiving the same response; after which he sprinkled the people with the blood of the sacrifice, saying: 'Behold the blood of the Covenant which Jahveh hath made with you concerning these words.'

In this way Abraham's seed entered into Covenant with Abraham's God. The old thought of fellowship effected by sacrifice is here enriched by a new element: the fellowship of Jahveh with His people is conditional upon their keeping His Law. What, then, was this Law given on Sinai? The original form is lost; though that given by J in Exodus xxxiv is older than the familiar version in chapter xx. Whatever the precise form, this primitive Law was something completely new. It dealt not only with the relations of man to God, but also with those of man to man. It declared that Jahveh was jealous, requiring the undivided allegiance of His people; and it forbad the use of images to represent Him. There is as yet no explicit claim that He is the only God; but He alone of tribal gods will brook no rival; He alone of tribal gods will allow no created thing, such as bull or calf, to serve as His symbol; for all creatures are finite, and '*I will be*' of the Hebrews wants to lead them on to a conception of Himself which knows no limits.

The simple commands and prohibitions which regulate social relations are no less novel, for they are *moral*. They declare that Jahveh's first requirement is moral righteousness, and they introduce a new conception of what constitutes its opposite. The most primitive conception of evil is that it is *zymotic*, something which works like leaven secretly and pervasively, and exhales from uncanny objects, such as dead bodies and things or persons under a curse. A man shuns evil of this kind as he would infectious disease, but he has no sense of moral responsibility for it: indeed, as we saw in the case of shed blood, the same thing under different circumstances might be definitely good. But the giving of the primitive Law made evil appear primarily as *sin*, that is man's deliberate disobedience to a known command of God; and this at once puts the emphasis in human life on to the right use of free-will, the faculty which it is the purpose of the Restoration to re-enthrone at the apex of our being. Long afterwards St. Paul discerned that the function of the Law was to act like a hot, stinging fomentation, drawing the all-pervading sinfulness of human nature up to the surface where it could be dealt with. When sinful man had learnt by bitter experience his inability to keep the Law, even when he would, then the time was ripe for God to act again. In this way the Law was our schoolmaster* to

---

* The word translated 'schoolmaster' is *paidagōgos* or pedagogue, literally a boy-leader. It meant originally the slave who took the child to the master for his lessons.

bring us to Christ; and of that Law, ever increasing like a rolling snowball through the centuries, the Ten Words given to Moses were the nucleus.

It was the possession of this unique moral Law, this essential connection of worship with conduct, that from Sinai onwards marked out the seed of Abraham as a people apart, slow as they were to recognise their separateness.

As God's instrument for the Restoration they had to be segregated in order to be educated; the Law once given must never be forgotten. To this end the stone tablets on which it was written were placed in a chest or Ark, and the Ark was kept in a special tent or Tabernacle, which moved with the camp and served as a centre of worship.

Thus the Ark and the Tabernacle together constituted a portable Bethel, an abiding pledge or sacrament of the Presence of God with His people, and a continual reminder of their Covenant obligations. In so far as the Chosen People were faithful to the Ten Words, they had a right to Jahveh's care and protection, a claim upon Him, founded in some sense on their own merit, which other peoples had not.

From Sinai the tribes made north, and reached the border of their inheritance, only to be turned back by their own unfaith. Years passed, and of the generation that had experienced the Exodus only three remained; but the new generation, wilderness born, was at last a nation. Avoiding the unfriendly territory of Edom, they passed through Moab, whither their fame had preceded them. The Gentile prophet Balaam was summoned in hot haste from beyond the Euphrates, in order that he might curse 'this people come out of Egypt.' Balaam knew that he ought not to go; but yielded to bribes. Finally from three successive mountain-tops, overborne by inspiration, he blessed them, to the horror of Balak who had sent for him; and looking down on Jacob encamped below, Balaam saw,

E

not them only but the Star and Sceptre which should proceed from them. It was given to the pagan seer first to know that Israel's history should culminate in a Person.

The mountains of Moab look straight across the Jordan into Canaan. Moses went up Mount Pisgah and saw the Land he might not enter. He who had hesitated at the burning bush had none the less brought his people out of Egypt, had been their prophet and Lawgiver and suffered for forty years their manners in the wilderness. Through these experiences the life so fought for and so menaced in infancy had come to vigorous old age. Now, with Israel on the borders of her inheritance, Moses was to lay down both his office and his life.

That was not the end. The great Deliverer was yet to stand upon another mountain within the Promised Land, and talk with the Star of Jacob Himself of 'the Exodus which *He* should accomplish at Jerusalem.'

CHAPTER VII

THE CHOSEN PEOPLE

(ii) From the Settlement of Canaan to the Division of the Kingdom

WHEN Joshua succeeded Moses in the leadership of the Chosen People he bore in his own name both an epitome of previous revelation and a pledge for the future,— *Jahveh is Salvation*. By the events of the last forty years Jahveh had shown His care for Israel to be that of a father for his firstborn, and had proved Himself to be their redeemer from bondage and at all times their shepherd. Through the agency of Moses He had further revealed that His essential requirement from His people was righteousness. Salvation, which includes both deliverance and providence, lay, therefore, in faithfulness to Him. But just as rain falls first on the surface of the ground and thence slowly percolates to lower levels, so the revelation received by the prophets took a long time to soak down to other people. Centuries were to pass before that which was as clear as the noonday to Moses himself really became part of the national consciousness.

The Land of Promise was not emptily awaiting its heirs; nor did its conquest, facilitated by the triumphs of the Ark at Jordan and Jericho, result in the complete dispossession of the Canaanites. After the isolation of the wilderness the Israelites found themselves living at close quarters with tribes whose language and customs were nearly related to their own.* The high places of

---

* Some of these were probably *Israelite* tribes who had never left Canaan, and, not having shared in the experience of the Exodus and of Sinai, were regarded by the entrants as inferior.

Canaan, some of them connected with theophanies to Israel's ancestors, had the traditional apparatus of Semitic worship; and lent themselves as readily to the worship of Jahveh as to that of Baal. There lay the danger. The Israelites were themselves as yet no more than henotheists; Jahveh, the 'El of Sinai, was their tribal God and Canaan was now His land, which in fulfilment of His ancient promise He had at last given into their hands. Once in Canaan, what more natural than to call Him Baal, the Owner of the land and the source of its fertility, and to think of Him as differing only in His superior strength from the lesser Baals whom He had evicted?

The trend of this conception of the deity, which starts by being henotheistic, is always in the direction of polytheism, because nature gods, besides being in any case non-moral and non-jealous, are inevitably thought of as having different spheres.

So this fusion with heathenism drew the Chosen People in the opposite direction from the ethical monotheism adumbrated at Sinai. Moreover the Baalim were represented in animal form; and the custom of representing Jahveh as a bull, the symbol of strength and of creative power, received fresh impetus, even if it did not actually originate at this time. On the other hand, the change from a nomadic to a settled life in contact with their fellow Semites brought some features into the religious life of Israel which were not evil. Now that they were farmers as well as shepherds, cereal offerings became customary in addition to libations and animal sacrifice; and three great agricultural feasts, traditional in Canaan, were added to the calendar, while the Sabbath became pre-eminently a day of rest from field labour for beast as well as man.*

* In J's. version of the original Law also, something of the duty of man to the lower creation is included: Thou shalt not seethe a kid in his mother's milk: a recognition of the fact that right relationship to the animals is integral to true religion.

Strong influences also were at work to preserve and foster true religion. Frequent inter-tribal wars threw the Chosen People back upon Jahveh as their sole defender; and the Ark, kept at Shiloh after the settlement, was an abiding witness to the Covenant. Nor was this all. It is at this time that we first hear of the *nebhî'îm*, who, whatever their limitations, were certainly zealots for Jahveh as against other gods, and also of the Nazirites, persons self-consecrated to Jahveh, wearing their hair unshorn as a token of their vow and abstaining from wine, the richest product of the land, because it figured so largely in the sensuous worship of Baal. Lastly there were the Judges. Joshua had no immediate successor in the sole leadership of Israel, but in every national crisis there was a man for the hour. As often as Israel endangered her separateness by compromise with heathenism and neglect of her moral obligations, so often was she in due course delivered over to heathen oppression. The champion, when he came, had not only to restore her liberty, but to lift again the standard of the disregarded Law.

At the end of the period of the Judges stands the giant figure of Samuel. He was himself a Judge, both in the more usual sense of an administrator of the law, and in that in which it is used of Gideon and Samson; and he was also a prophet. Like John the Baptist centuries later, he came at a time when the voice of prophecy had long been silent, and religion was at a low ebb: also like the Baptist, he was dedicated to God from his mother's womb.

He grew up with the keepers of the Ark at Shiloh,— 'priests' they are called, but the functions later accounted specifically priestly were not as yet peculiar to them,—and as a child foretold the catastrophe in which subsequently the Ark was lost. Those awful months when the Ark was in the hands of the Philistines at last brought home to Israel the truth demonstrated by every earlier disaster.

Jahveh and Israel were in covenant; Jahveh would fight for them only if they kept His laws. To use the pledge of His Presence as if it were a charm that acted irrespectively of His Will was presumption, and could only bring worse punishment. In this elementary way this unformed people had to learn by experience that *God is true.* His actions must always be consistent with His character; and naughty and impenitent children cannot be treated as if they were good.

The way was now open for radical reformation; and Samuel, whose fame as a prophet had spread over the land, was its acknowledged leader. For the rest of his long life he 'judged' Israel, hearing cases as Moses had done in the wilderness, and going round in circuit to do so. In this way the long-neglected moral law was applied to life; and precedents were established, based on its principles, which themselves in time became law and were known together with the original decalogue as the Law of Moses.

This process, closely akin to that by which our English Common Law was evolved, had doubtless begun before the time of Samuel and continued after it for the rest of Israel's history.

Samuel showed his leadership in his willingness to use other people. He saw in the *nebhî'îm* a potency for good and organised them into bands,—'sons of the prophets' who, probably through comparison with himself, were little thought of, but served a useful and patriotic purpose. It is quite likely that we owe the beginnings of Israel's sacred literature to these prophetic schools.

Under Samuel, for the first time since Joshua, the Chosen People found themselves under one leader who acted both as ruler and prophet. The supreme ruler was Jahveh; but Samuel, like Joshua and Moses before him, was the go-between. It was a short step from this sort of leadership to actual monarchy; and the oldest tradition which tells of Saul's search for his father's asses and subsequent anointing by Samuel, suggests that Samuel himself favoured the institution of the monarchy, and saw nothing in it incompatible with the theocracy. Later, when the nation was embittered by bad kings, there grew up a tradition that Samuel had foretold all along that kings would be a curse rather than a blessing. Whichever view is correct, the monarchy looks to Samuel as its founder.

The reigns of the three kings of undivided Israel occupied about a century, at the end of which time the nation was at the zenith of its outward prosperity. Saul, beginning nobly, repulsed the Philistines on the western frontier, but through his inability to obey at a crisis proved himself unworthy to found the royal house. No son of his succeeded him, but David, bred among sheep on the Bethlehem hills. David's service to Israel is hard to estimate. He embodied for them the ideal of the theocratic king, the prince who acts for God. He gave them a capital, wresting the almost impregnable Jerusalem from the hands of the Jebusites, and made it the holiest of their holy places by bringing the Ark into it. By his own gift of song he founded the psalmody peculiar to his people, and ever afterwards connected with his name. His very sins are made precious by his penitence. No wonder that the promised blessing of all nations should henceforward be looked for, not in Abraham's seed at large, but in the house and lineage of David. The idea of the Messiah, or Anointed One, Jahveh's earthly vice-regent, first suggested by what David actually was, became from this time onwards the focus of Israel's hope.

The reign of Solomon effected both the consummation of the political work of Saul and David, and a radical change for the worse in the life of the nation. So manifoldly wise that all subsequent wisdom was put under his name, and cleaving at first to his father's ideals, Solomon built in Jerusalem a permanent abode for the Ark upon the traditional site of the sacrifice of Isaac. The Temple was at once the chief, though not as yet the only sanctuary. It was the Bethel of bethels, unrivalled in splendour. Further, by conquest and development of trade Solomon made Israel first among her neighbours, with territory stretching from Hamath to the Red Sea. At the same time he ruined the simplicity of her earlier life, and opened upon her once more the floodgates of heathen influence.

At this point we need to remind ourselves that we study the history of the Chosen People because it is the history of the building of the bridge between God and fallen man. As a bridge is made of stones, so is a nation of individuals; the Chosen People were not themselves the bridge so much as the quarry whence it was hewn; and as in Eden, so always the Devil competes with God for every man's allegiance. Each soul is a battlefield; on it is fought out in microcosm the elemental conflict between Light and Darkness, in which the determining factor is free-will, and since the race is a unity, no one can possibly foresee the consequences of his own fidelity or lack of it. The recorded history of the Chosen People, like all history, is general and largely external. It is dominated by great individuals in whom the progress of the Divine purpose comes to the surface and is visible; but for the most part the bridge, like the seed, grows secretly. We know that we owe Moses to his mother's courage, we know something of the pious influences that moulded Samuel; but the bridge was built very largely of stones hidden from the eye, like the seven thousand in Elijah's time of whom he himself had no knowledge until God told him. When, later still, Isaiah formulated his doctrine of the faithful remnant through whom the hope of Israel should be realised, he was only putting into words something which had been a fact from the beginning, and was already symbolised in the story of Noah and the Ark. Abraham himself was the flower of this hidden faithfulness to the best that was known in ancient times. It is like the underground stem of a virile plant, sending up shoots at intervals, which may not always overtop the weeds among which they grow, but will never fail to bear fruit.

With this in mind we approach the jungle of the kings of Israel and Judah.

CHAPTER VIII

THE CHOSEN PEOPLE

(iii) Israel and Judah

THE oppression and misery of Solomon's latter days had been such that either reformation or revolt was bound to follow his death. His son, Rehoboam, having his father's vices without his virtues, and acting as oriental despot rather than a theocratic king, precipitated revolt. In consequence the ten tribes who held the fertile uplands of the north, with the great trade-routes running through, were established under an upstart of the name of Jeroboam, while David's degenerate grandson in the barren and sequestered territory of Judah and Benjamin retained Jerusalem *and* the Hope. Jeroboam, seeing that he would lose the allegiance of his people if they continued to go to Jerusalem to worship, established a bull image of Jahveh at each of the two ancient shrines of Dan and Bethel; and these, conveniently situated at either end of the kingdom, became under priests of his own appointment the centres of Israel's worship.

The narrative in Kings, presupposing that Jerusalem was in Jeroboam's time the one legitimate sanctuary, and also that the priesthood was already restricted to the tribe of Levi, reprobates his conduct accordingly. In the eyes of his contemporaries this part of it was probably far less heinous; but there is no getting over the bull images, and those shrines were indeed the source of much of the evil, all of which is laid in retrospect at the door of 'Jeroboam, the son of Nebat who made Israel to sin.'

The main interest of the history of the two kingdoms, often at war but sometimes in alliance against common enemies, lies at first in the North. There was at the beginning no ordered succession to the kingship. As in the latter days of the Roman Empire, the general whose success in war won him the most popular favour hacked his way to the throne, and few of these self-made kings died in their beds. Even the house of Omri, who built Samaria as the capital and partly restored the political prosperity lost at the disruption, saw only three generations before it was wiped out by Jehu, whose own dynasty after four reigns met the same fate. Omri's son Ahab married a forceful Tyrian princess, and under her influence attempted to make the Tyrian Baal the national god. Popular ideas of Jahveh were so debased and His worship so like that of Baal that to many the change must have seemed slight. Elijah alone saw that the difference between Jahveh of Israel and Baal of Tyre was as that of light from darkness, and found a way to act. There is no more splendid display of faith in all history than the scene on Carmel, crowned at last by the fire from heaven. Elijah is a strange, stern figure, like a Semitic *nabhi* in his ecstasy and reaction, and like John the Baptist in his fearless faith, appearing from nowhere and vanishing yet more mysteriously; but he saved the faith given on Sinai, and he made an impression on the Chosen People which has never been effaced. Later generations felt that the glorious future to which they looked forward could not be realised without his help; and to this day, when the rite of Circumcision is performed in a Jewish household, with all the modern equipment of sterilised instruments and even anaesthetics, an empty chair is set for Elijah the Prophet, who saved the Chosen People from losing their vocation.

The most constant factor in the history of the Northern kingdom was Syria. No geographic boundary divided them, and the two powers were almost always at strife. In the time of Elijah's great and gentle successor Elisha,

Samaria was itself encompassed by a Syrian army, which withdrew at a false alarm only when the besieged were at the last extremity. Syria had, however, other enemies besides Israel. Away to the north-east, beyond the great river, lay Assyria, then approaching the zenith of her strength. Once Syria came to death-grips with this stronger foe she had no time to play beggar-my-neighbour with Israel over frontier cities.

A nation constantly at war has at least no time to grow soft, but before the middle of the eighth century, when Jeroboam II, the fourth of Jehu's line was on the throne, a generation had grown up in Israel which had not known war. Failing entirely to see that Israel herself must be Assyria's next victim when Syria fell, they interpreted the material prosperity consequent on the cessation of Syrian hostilities as a sign of Jahveh's favour, and lavish in their offerings and regular in attendance at His feasts, spoke with glib confidence of the approaching 'Day of the Lord,' when His goodness towards His Chosen People should be displayed yet further. This light self-satisfied worship was not religion for it did not bind. The moral law was forgotten, the priests at the shrines who should have been its exponents were themselves sunk in bribery and lust; the rich trading class lived in luxury and vice, and the oppressed poor had no man to pity them. The name of Jahveh was worshipped indeed, but the character or rather the lack of it associated with the Name was that of heathen Baal.

Into this Vanity Fair of the Northern Kingdom came Christian and Faithful in the persons of Amos and Hosea. On the bleak mountains south of Jerusalem the old pastoral life still persisted; and Amos the herdsman of Tekoa, like Moses of old and other shepherds afterwards on the same hills, had his theophany when he was watching his flocks. Next time he went up to Bethel to sell his wool, he delivered his message. The gist of it was that the Northern

Kingdom was rotten to the core and completely self-deluded; and that the 'Day of the Lord' which they anticipated so confidently would be a day not of triumph but of disaster. They would shortly be conquered and taken captive to Assyria, and no more would be left of them than the fragments of a lion's meal, 'two legs and a piece of an ear.'

Ejected from Bethel and gaining no general audience, Amos must have found refuge in a small circle of the faithful,* where his prophecies were committed to writing; and so, somewhat disarranged but as vivid as when they were spoken they have come down through twenty-eight centuries to us.

Perhaps twenty years after the first appearance of Amos, Hosea received his message through the tragedy of his own life. His wife, a product of the corrupt civilisation of the time, was unfaithful to him, and finally in the language of our own day went on the streets. When she had sold herself into slavery in order to live, Hosea, who had never ceased to love her, bought her back and took her again for his wife. Then he saw that Jahveh felt about Israel as he felt about Gomer. If something of the old pagan idea of the Baal as the husband of his people and so the source of their fruitfulness lay behind his thought, it is but another instance of the principle of Cana, for with him it becomes the vehicle of a new revelation. Hosea is the first of all the prophets to declare the *love* of God, and he racks the resources of human language to do so.

Amos and Hosea were primarily champions of the forgotten teaching of Moses, that Jahveh is righteous and requires righteousness; but there are some developments.

---

* The document E in the Pentateuch is thought by many critics to have come from this small section of the nation under the influence of Amos and Hosea. It certainly emanates from the Northern Kingdom.

Amos sees Him as ruling the heathen nations as well as Israel, and judging each according to its own standard which is emphatically not hers. He calls Jahveh Lord of Sabaoth, of Hosts, in the sense that all earthly armies can be instruments of His purpose, as the Assyrian army is shortly to be in regard to Israel, who, just because she is the Chosen People and ought to have known better, will receive, not as she expected more honour and glory, but much heavier punishment than the nations whose gods are simply nothings. Amos is thus a *practical* monotheist, and the express theory was soon to follow.

Hosea, himself an Israelite and loving Israel as Amos did not, gives the same message much more tenderly. More clearly too than Amos he discerns that Jahveh's wrath is motived by love, and looks forward beyond the judgment to a glorious future.* His language in speaking of this blessed future of restored fellowship with Jahveh is so like that used elsewhere about the Messianic Kingdom that it cannot be disassociated from it, though he makes no express mention of the Messiah himself. He sees also to the root of Israel's evil,—that it is lack of true knowledge of God which results in the neglect of the moral law bewailed by Amos. As we saw at the outset, religion is faith issuing in conduct; and the faith of the Chosen People is built upon the revelation that God is Himself righteous, and requires righteousness in His people,—a truth graphically conveyed by Amos in the figure of the plumbline dropped against the crooked wall. Imperfect knowledge of God always results in an imperfect moral standard; and there are plenty of instances in history as flagrant as Israel: the mediaeval knight who could attend Mass in his own chapel while his enemy starved in the dungeon below; the men of our own nation who, even in the last century could offer thanks to God on deck for the good haul of slaves then suffocating in the hold.

* Amos also has a hopeful epilogue, but it may be a later addition.

At about the same time that Jeroboam II began to reign in Israel, Uzziah, eighth in line from Rehoboam mounted the throne of Judah as a lad of sixteen. After reigning successfully and well for some years he was stricken with leprosy and spent the rest of his life shut up in a lazar-house while his son Jotham acted as regent. When at last he was known to be dead, many must have pondered the contrast between his end and his beginning.

One day of that same year in which the instability of earthly glory had been so signally demonstrated, a young man of Jerusalem named Isaiah, attending worship in the Temple as usual, saw beyond it to the glory and worship of heaven. He saw Jahveh 'high and lifted up,' asking for human helpers, and, overwhelmed with the sense of his own and his people's sinfulness, he offered himself and was accepted.

Everything in his subsequent message sprang from what he learnt that day,—the consuming holiness of Jahveh, Ruler of the hosts of heaven as well as those of earth.

Isaiah was a statesman prophet in no easy times. Religiously things were little better in Judah than in Israel, and idolatry was rampant. Politically the eastern empires were in the melting pot, and Judah, too weak to stand alone, everybody's prey and in everybody's way, looked around fearfully for an ally. Isaiah, foreseeing the fall of both kingdoms and a better beyond, bade them trust in God and wait; but could not prevent Ahaz from becoming the vassal of Assyria. With the accession of Hezekiah some measure of reform was possible; and the pillars which now served to link the worship of Jahveh with the unprogressive Semitic heathenism, whence it had sprung and with which it was surrounded, were removed from the Temple.

In 722 after a terrible siege, Samaria fell, as Amos, Hosea and Isaiah had all foretold; and the bulk of the population of the Northern Kingdom was deported to other parts of the Assyrian Empire, there to lose for ever their national identity.*

By this disaster Judah was deprived of her only buffer against the iron might of Assyria; but still Isaiah, motived always by the unchangeable truth that he had seen in the Temple, counselled trust. The time for Judah's fall was not yet: till it came Jahveh could and did turn back the enemy provoked by Judah's revolt and alliance with Egypt, from the very walls of Jerusalem.

Isaiah perished at last in the heathen reaction under Manasseh, still upheld, surely, by the vision of the Lord, 'high and lifted up.'

All the main points of the teaching of Amos and Hosea are emphasised and developed by Isaiah and his lesser contemporary, Micah. The truth of Jahveh's utter dependability is reinforced by that of His transcendent holiness; and the hope of the Messianic Kingdom under a worthy scion of David becomes with both prophets more definite and detailed. From the stem,—that is, the old dry tree stump,—of Jesse there shall yet come a shoot, under whose rule men shall be at peace with God, with each other and with the lower creation. This blessed future is, however, not for all. Isaiah sees more clearly than any prophet before him that the real Chosen People is not the nation at large, but only those members of it who are individually faithful amid the general apostasy. In his latter days Isaiah himself became, as Amos and Hosea always were, one of a small and often persecuted minority. Within such a circle consciousness of the value of the

---

* Some years later the desolated territory of Israel was re-populated by Assyrian colonists. These were troubled by lions who had grown bold in the absence of men; and believing this to be a sign of the wrath of Jahveh against the strangers in the land, they complained to the Assyrian King, who sent back an Israelite priest to teach them to worship Jahveh! The descendants of these colonists by intermarriage with the few Israelites remaining were thus mongrels both in race and religion,—the Samaritans of later times.

individual was necessarily quickened, not indeed so as to rule out the idea of the all-importance of the nation, but as its complementary truth, out of which much was to grow. It is true that Isaiah seems to expect the golden age to follow immediately on the coming judgment. He is like a man gazing at a far-distant mountain, which in the clear atmosphere appears quite near. Actually the fulfilment of the Messianic prophecies began at the Incarnation, and is still moving forward to its consummation.

After the fall of the Northern Kingdom in 722, the sole hope for the fulfilment of the promise made to Abraham rested with Judah. The work of Amos and Hosea did not, however, perish with the Kingdom; for the faithful remnant of Judah was reinforced by refugees from Israel, bringing with them the northern document E, which was combined with the southern J in Judah, probably during the idolatrous reigns of Manasseh and Amon. This subterranean literary activity of the true servants of Jahveh at times when His worship was corrupt and proscribed is a characteristic of the history from this time onwards, and was of untold value both to themselves and to subsequent generations. Such men were the vestal virgins of revelation, guarding between their hands the flickering flame which was one day to enlighten the world.

Their influence must surely also have moulded the little Josiah. Grandson of Manasseh* who introduced Assyrian star-worship into the very Temple and, like Ahaz before him, offered one of his children in the fire to Moloch, son of that Amon who was so vile that his own servants slew him, Josiah ascending the throne at the age of eight was a life-long servant of Jahveh. By the time he had reached manhood the decline of Assyria had laid Judah

---

* A much later tradition than Kings II says that Manasseh died repentant. However this may be, he and Amon as well as Josiah were among our Lord's ancestors.

open to the attack of the fierce Scythians from the north; and at this juncture a trio of prophets appeared to restore the panic-stricken people to their senses. The greatest of these, Jeremiah, began at this time a ministry which was to last forty years and witness the fulfilment of all the prophecies of judgment. He was naturally diffident and sensitive, and for most of this time stood practically alone among a people who hated his message and misjudged his motive. At the time of his call he was bidden to look at an almond tree growing near by. The Hebrew for almond tree is *shāqēd*, which is almost identical in sound with *shōqēd*, I am watching over. How often in after years must pink blossom against blue sky have reminded Jeremiah of Jahveh's *truth* and so helped him also to be true.

One day, about five years after this, the king's secretary, Shaphan, showed him a book which the priest Hilkiah had found in the Temple. The Temple was then under repair, and Hilkiah seems to have found the book when he was turning out lumber-rooms to find money to pay the workmen. This book was beyond all doubt the main part of our Deuteronomy; and its discovery prompted a reformation in Judah which had far-reaching effects. The name of the author is unknown; but he was probably one of the Temple priests who belonged to the prophetic faithful remnant, and wrote his book during the reign of Manasseh and hid it in the Temple against better times. Then he died,—perhaps a martyr's death, and the book was forgotten until Hilkiah found it.

The 'Second Law' is so called because it consists of a series of discourses put into the mouth of Moses at the end of the wanderings, and purporting to be his final instructions to the Chosen People for their life in Canaan. We have already seen how all the outgrowth of the primitive law was attributed indiscriminately to the first great law-giver, and as this book embodies and expands much of the JE code, its Mosaic form, far from being a deception, was the natural one for the author to choose. In spirit, however, Deuteronomy shows great advance, for it is imbued with the teaching of the eighth century prophets. The relation of Jahveh to His people is one of *Love:* as He showed His for them in the events of the wilderness and the Exodus, so must they show theirs for Him in obedience to His Law. Worship, social relations, relations with the lower creation are all to spring from love. In regard to worship the laws are rigorous: the Deuteronomist, taught by his own times, sees that the only possible way to keep religion pure is to have but one sanctuary for sacrifice, and to allow only the Levites to minister at it. As we saw in the case of Dan and Bethel, the local sanctuaries were always the door through which heathenism got in. Though the one sanctuary is nowhere named in Deuteronomy, it could obviously be no other than Jerusalem which, though not an ancient shrine, had from the first a peculiar importance as possessing both Ark and Temple, and had grown still further in prestige since its wonderful deliverance from the Assyrian host in 701. The history of the Levitical priesthood is obscure, but it is quite likely that Moses himself put the Ark and Tabernacle at once into the care of his brother Aaron and his family, and that after the Settlement many of the priests who kept the various shrines were appointed from the same tribe. The offering of sacrifice, however, was the right of every man, and was by no means monopolised by these priests, though they did perform it. The restriction of sacrifice to the Temple priesthood and the Temple was the main feature of the Deuteronomic reformation, though it seems that priests from the local shrines who were Levites had equal rights with the Temple priests themselves if they came to Jerusalem.

It is hard to realise what it meant at one stroke to sweep away all heathen altars and emblems, and to abolish the local sanctuaries, and to dispossess the priests, nor how strong must have been the popular feeling that could effect it. The change this wrought in the life of the people was very great. As long as sacrifice might be offered by anybody the slaughter of animals for food had always been a quasi-religious act; now that it was restricted to the capital, and dwellers in outlying parts went up only to the three great annual feasts, sacrifice though still central ceased to be a frequent element in worship. At the same time the newly-found book was made the basis of solemn renewal of the Covenant, so that the study of the Law tended to take the place in popular religion formerly occupied by sacrifice. This reformation, which must at first have brought joy to the prophets, seems soon to have become perverted. The Temple priests who had grown more in importance than in spirituality by the abolition of the local shrines, laid almost exclusive stress on outward observance; and Jeremiah, still preaching repentance and the imminence of doom, found himself in lonely opposition to the priestly and patriotic party imbued with this legalistic spirit. In his isolation he came to develop still further the doctrine of the individual, to see that each man must somehow ultimately bear the punishment of his own sins; and also, in face of the seeming failure of the old covenant to produce a holy people, to look forward dimly to a better covenant in the future.

Meanwhile a crisis of the nations was approaching. The fall of Nineveh, the Assyrian capital, in 612 left her some-time vassal Babylon at strife with Egypt for the mastery of Western Asia. In 605 the issue was decided in favour of Babylon at Carchemish, and Judah became a vassal of the new power. Futile revolt, in spite of Jeremiah's warnings brought speedy vengeance: in 597 Nebuchadnez-zar himself took Jerusalem, stripped the Temple, and took the reigning king, Josiah's grandson Jehoiachim, together with the pride of the people captive to Babylon. The Day of the Lord had come.

Jeremiah, left behind with the riff-raff under a puppet king, now entered on the final phase of his life-long passion. We know what his companions were like from his own terrible figure of the rotten figs. From their shattered faith in the inviolability of Jerusalem they turned again to idolatry; and the Temple became once more a pantheon of heathenism. Jeremiah lived on, knowing that the worst was yet to come; that within ten years city and Temple alike would be utterly destroyed.

There is a strange legend in the second book of Maccabees which relates that when this catastrophe was imminent, Jeremiah took the sacred Ark out of the Temple and hid it in a cave in one of the mountains of Moab, the same from which Moses had viewed the Promised Land, and foretold that it should remain hidden 'until the time that God gather His people again together and receive them unto mercy.' There it may still be: who knows?

Meanwhile the hope of the future was with the Exiles.

CHAPTER IX

THE CHOSEN PEOPLE

(iv) Exile, Return and Restoration*

WHEN the captain of the Babylonian guard went round Jerusalem collecting captives, he did not enquire who had been faithful to Jahveh and who had not. He chose those who would contribute something to the land of their exile,—'the craftsmen and the smiths.' Consequently the contingent of the seed of Abraham that was thus marched off to the land of their origin did not all react to their circumstances in the same way. No wholesale conversion resulted from the shock of deportation: many indeed were hardened by it and forsook the faith of Jahveh altogether. Others had absorbed the teaching of the prophets sufficiently to believe that Jahveh was loving and the punishment just; but the conception of Jahveh as the national God had been strengthened by the establishment of Jerusalem as the one sanctuary, and there can have been few, if any, among the exiles who did not feel that banishment from Jerusalem was also banishment from Him.

Once in Babylon, the exiles seem to have had their own quarters and to have been free to do almost anything except go home. They may have been harshly treated at times, but they were never slaves as their forefathers had been in Egypt.

Their intense homesickness, combined with the knowledge that it was dalliance with heathenism that had brought them there, made the faithful, at any rate, cleave close

---

* Restoration is used here in its usual sense of the re-establishment of the Chosen People in their own land, not in the wider sense explained in the Introduction.

together, and strive to maintain their separateness by such religious observance as was possible on foreign soil. Sacrifice, of course, there could not be, but customs such as the Sabbath, the food law and prayer offered towards Jerusalem were practised with new fervour, and the historical and legal records which they had brought with them assumed a new importance.

Their first meetings for prayer and study were probably on river banks or in private houses: then as they became established they erected each group its special building,— the meeting-house or synagogue which was to play so large a part in their life from this time forward. The Exile had acted like an earthquake in the lives of these people, upsetting all previous ideas and raising a host of agonising problems;* and it was in the synagogues of Babylon that they found themselves and began again.

About five years after the exiles had come to Babylon, the priest Ezekiel, who was of their number, was called to be a prophet. He had a mysterious symbolic vision by the river Chebar,—probably one of the canals,—of the chariot of God; and the impression it conveyed to him was that Jahveh Whom they mostly thought of as localised at Jerusalem had *come to visit* His people where they were, and that He was the One, transcendent, omnipresent God of all the earth. After this he was told to prophesy that both Jerusalem and the Temple would shortly be destroyed. His fellow exiles who still held that Jahveh's honour was bound up with His Holy City, refused to listen to him; and Ezekiel was obliged to deliver his message in dumb show, as by making a mud model of Jerusalem, and knocking it down with pebbles.

In 587 his prophecy was fulfilled. The puppet king having tried to rebel, a Babylonian army destroyed both Temple and City, and deported a second contingent of captives to Babylon.

* e.g. The origin of evil and the meaning of suffering.

This overwhelming catastrophe was a turning-point in the lives of the exiles, and not least in that of Ezekiel himself. After the fulfilment of his prophecy he had a humbler people to deal with, and one which had abandoned for ever the idea of Jahveh as a merely national God. They had grasped at last both the teaching of Moses, that Jahveh's essential nature and requirement was righteousness, and the lofty monotheism of the later prophets. They saw that their national ingratitude and disobedience had merited the Exile, but they believed also that the same holiness of Jahveh which had necessitated the punishment would also necessitate their restoration. The honour of His Name was bound up with His people, and He could not cast them off for ever.

Ezekiel's later prophecies are very interesting because they combine old elements with new, and the priestly outlook with the prophetic. He goes further than Jeremiah in regard to the individual, not only in maintaining that in the long run it is the sinner himself who suffers for his sins, but in his insistence on the need of personal faith and repentance. He takes up the old prophetic hope of the Messianic Kingdom, and depicts it minutely in terms of the priestly ideal: the life of the holy nation is to centre in the one visible sanctuary and find expression and safeguard in an ordered round of worship. The establishment and maintenance of this ideal kingdom is pre-eminently the Act of Jahveh Himself, by which He will declare His Holiness to the nations though there is no thought as yet that the nations will share His Kingdom. The deliverer through whom the Kingdom is to be set up is spoken of as Jahveh Himself and as the Davidic prince almost in a breath, though the two are never specifically identified; but the power that alone can make Israel the holy nation she was always meant to be and never yet had been is Jahveh's Spirit. This promise of the Spirit is a new note in prophecy, characteristic of this period, and finds its most wonderful expression in the vision of the Valley of Dry Bones. Ezekiel was beginning to see that, as Jeremiah had already suggested, the Mosaic Covenant could never of itself bring in the glorious future: somehow or other it had got to be superseded and Jahveh must Himself effect the redemption from sin which His people could not accomplish for themselves. The Law was beginning to fulfil its office of pedagogue to lead men to Christ.

The priestly ideals embodied in Ezekiel's later visions were peculiar to himself. The exiles were firmly convinced that as the root of all their past evil had been neglect of the Law, so now their only hope for the future lay in its strict observance.

'The Former Prophets,'—Joshua, Judges, Samuel, and Kings,—were, as we saw, compiled at this time from the Deuteronomic standpoint, as was also the Priestly Code which in relation to its own time can now be appreciated. It is really a collection of the traditions and rules of the priesthood, combined with an historical survey, in which the author traces the origin of all religious institutions to the earliest times. This ignorance of the law of development makes P as valuable an authority for its own time as it is valueless for any other. Begun about the time of Ezekiel's death (c. 572), the work was continued well into the next century, by different hands, no doubt, but with such unity of style and spirit that the author is always spoken of in the singular. The earliest part of it is the Law of Holiness contained in Leviticus xvii to xxvi, and known by the symbol H. Like the rest of the document, H contains material from different eras. The ruling idea, as with Ezekiel, is that the people of Jahveh are a holy nation and that their holiness culminates in the priesthood, which is now limited to the family of Aaron.* As to what

* Ezekiel limits it to the family of Zadok, himself a descendant of Aaron, who was the priest in David's time.

constitutes holiness, the thought in P is mixed. Though there is a great deal about real moral offences due to voluntary disobedience, there is quite as much about uncleanness which is contracted involuntarily through evil contacts. As has already been noted, the most primitive conception of evil is that it is zymotic, and as such involves no moral responsibility. If we believe that the whole universe is in some way involved in the consequences of the Fall, we cannot deny that this sort of evil exists; but the fact remains that only *moral* evil which proceeds from the will is actually *sin*, and that from sin, whether in angel or man or both, all other evil has resulted. Sin, therefore, is what has to be dealt with. P's conception of what constitutes human holiness is imperfect because it does not clearly differentiate between evil which is moral and that which is not. Nevertheless, the Priestly Code does from first to last put holiness in its right place as Jahveh's essential requirement from man; and all the observances which it ordains are directed to that end. Circumcision becomes for the first time the mark of the separateness of the holy seed from other nations. Ceremonial washings or baptisms are prescribed for the removal of defilement, and always preceded the sprinkling of sacrificial blood, so that later generations believed the original Covenant at Sinai to have been effected by those three means,—Circumcision, Baptism, and Sacrifice, and enjoined the same for the admission of proselytes. Lastly, the whole sacrificial system in P, while retaining the old material of sacrifice as well as the old ideas about the connection of life with blood, expresses a new conception of propitiation. Now that the holiness of God is at last the foundation-stone of faith, it is recognised that the only barrier to fellowship with Him lies on the side of man. The old idea of coaxing the Deity out of His unaccountable anger has disappeared: to propitiate now means to obtain forgiveness and so restore Covenant relationship. This new-born sense of sin finds its fullest expression in the rites of the Day of Atonement, formulated at this time and put into practice after the Return. Priests, people, and the sanctuary itself were first purified from evil by the blood of sacrifice: then the sins of the people were confessed over the head of a live goat which, thus burdened, was driven into the wilderness, never to return. No one knows how this practice originated, nor what is meant by saying that the scapegoat is 'for Azazel.' There may be an ancient heathen rite behind it, and in later Jewish literature Azazel is the name of an evil angel. The rites of the Day of Atonement were valuable, not for their origin but for what they expressed and foreshadowed. When people began to realise, however dimly, that the main business of life was to get rid of sin, the process of Restoration in the wide sense was indeed progressing.

Ezekiel had been in his grave and the compilation of the Priestly Code some twenty years in progress before there appeared any practical likelihood of the exiles' return. Away to the north-east of Babylon lay the territory of the Medes and Persians, two Aryan tribes which had come originally from the shores of the Caspian Sea. Hitherto the Medes had maintained ascendancy over the Persians, but at this juncture the Persian prince Cyrus reversed that situation, and with a strong nation at his back marched against the allies of Babylon in Asia Minor, chief among whom was Croesus, King of Lydia.

About the time of this first hint of menace to their captors, one of the exiles began to prophesy. Nobody knows his name or anything about him; but as his prophecies were afterwards written without further title on the same roll with those of Isaiah of Jerusalem, he is called for convenience the Second-Isaiah. Chapter xl to lv are mostly his work, and perhaps the remaining ten at a later date. Second-Isaiah is unique among the prophets. He begins where they leave off. To him the Return is imminent, and though, like Isaiah of Jerusalem he sees in it the necessary step to a new and glorious age, and like Ezekiel proclaims it to be pre-eminently the Act of Jahveh Himself, he declares that it will be brought about through the human agency, not of a scion of David, but of the heathen prince Cyrus; and that the purpose of Israel's restoration is the enlightenment of all nations, not merely the vindication before them of Jahveh's love for His own. Thus Second-Isaiah makes plain the purpose of Israel's existence, already adumbrated in the third promise to Abraham, but never before clearly stated by the prophets, nor ever yet fully grasped by the Chosen People as a whole, whether Jewish or Christian. He does more. He reveals not only the purpose of Israel's restoration but also its method. The true Israel, the faithful remnant to which he addresses himself as to a corporate personality, is the servant of Jahveh for the fulfilment of His purpose for the world in a higher sense than is the unconscious Cyrus, for they have been fitted by the suffering of the Exile to be His willing though still imperfect instrument. In among many passages which express this thought there are four others known as the Servant Songs which have been called 'the most important page in the Old Testament for the study of the New.'

All sorts of historical and critical problems centre round these songs, and there is a vast literature on the subject. We see them inevitably in the light of their fulfilment in the Gospel, and cannot tell exactly what they meant to the prophet and his contemporaries, nor how they arose. It is simplest to take them first as still referring to the corporate personality of Israel and see what they add to that conception.

The Servant is represented in these songs first as the patient teacher of true religion to the Gentiles; then it appears that the discharge of his mission involves him in suffering, in which he is upheld by his utter confidence in God Who called him,—in other words, by believing *in* God as dependable Reality. Finally the unmerited suffering of the Servant voluntarily endured is seen to culminate in death, by means of which those for whom and at whose hands he suffers are restored to fellowship with Jahveh and he himself 'prolongs his days.' Thus the Servant is a victim, himself spotless as are the sacrificial lambs, and like them offered for the sins of others, but with this difference that he willingly offers himself, thus combining priestly and prophetic ideals of righteousness in a death which is at once sacrifice and personal moral act. The Servant as offerer of his own sacrifice transforms and sublimates all previous ideas of sacrifice existent among men. He reverses all human values by showing that suffering, which is in itself evil, and death which for man is the consequence of the Fall, are when taken hold of and used by the obedient will of man the very material of redemption, and therefore the most precious things in the world. The pains of death thus endured become the birth-pangs of new life, both for him who dies and for those for whom he dies. This picture of the Suffering Servant of Jahveh means far more than the prophet knew or we know, for it unveils the Heart of God Himself, in Whom sacrifice apart from sin exists eternally, acting in His restoration of the fallen world on a method consonant with His Own Being. It shows us that the only way in which evil can be got rid of is by making it instrumental to good; and that this can be effected only by the right use of suffering. When you suffer, as you must do, whether you will or not, everything depends upon how you take it. You can make it multiply evil, or you can make it good in itself and productive of more good. The root of the matter is faith and love and obedience.

Whatever the precise origin of the idea of the Servant, it is certain that it could not have arisen before the Exile. As individual consciousness grew, the theory that one suffered for the sins of one's ancestors ceased to satisfy; nor was the idea that for the individual the punishment always fitted the crime any longer tenable, for in the Exile the innocent had suffered with the guilty. To the problem of, 'Why do the righteous suffer?' the Suffering Servant is the answer. To the Jews he meant and still means the Chosen People suffering for and from the nations; and it is certain that he was never in pre-Christian thought identified with the individual Messiah. Yet in the last and greatest of the Songs of the Servant he is already an individual, for he is spoken of as being stricken 'for the transgressions of My people.' Thus the thought is contracted to Him in Whom the Chosen People at once fulfils its purpose of being the agent of redemption for the world, and is itself redeemed.

In 538 Cyrus, having conquered Lydia, returned on Babylon, diverted a canal in the night and walked in under the city gate. Shortly afterwards he issued an edict allowing and encouraging the Jews to return to Palestine; but only a small proportion of the colony took advantage of it. It was fifty years since the Second Deportation, sixty since the first; few remembered Jerusalem and the Temple, and most of them were doing very well where they were.

Those who stayed did not, however, become absorbed into the nations around them as the Northern Israelites had done, but remained Jews,—the nucleus of the Diaspora or Dispersion of the Chosen People which figures so largely in later history.

Those who returned took with them as the fruit of the Exile belief in Jahveh as the One and Only God; they were led conjointly by a priest and a prince, and were inspired both by Ezekiel's vision of the holy seed as a sacerdotal society, and by Second-Isaiah's doctrine of its world-mission, but the former predominated. They treasured the Scriptures, but no longer spoke the language in which they were written, for sixty years in Babylon had made Chaldaean the vernacular.

When at last they reached Jerusalem their first act was to erect an altar in the ruined Temple Court, and inaugurate daily sacrifice. It was a splendid act of faith and good intention, but the conditions of their life were a sore tax on perseverance. The rebuilding of the Temple was begun; and then discontinued for twelve years, first because the Samaritans, refused a share in the work, made mischief at the Persian Court, and then because no one had the heart to go on with it. That it was at last finished in 516 was largely due to the efforts of Haggai and Zechariah, two prophets who dealt in a very different manner with the same situation,—the one with blunt directness, the other with arresting symbolism, both stirring to action a stagnant and disillusioned people.

Perhaps half a century later the old prophetic ideas were voiced again by Malachi, whose name, 'My Messenger' was probably adopted to veil the identity of one called to rebuke the sins of the ruling class. He may well have prepared for the reformation inaugurated by Ezra, who arrived about 458 with a fresh caravan of exiles and the now completed Priestly Code. The priestly ideals were thenceforward rigorously enforced, and in default of a king the High Priest became the virtual head of the nation.

Thus the fifth century passed and the fourth dawned. The Davidic monarchy had not been restored and the glorious future had not come. The Chosen People were now a Church rather than a nation. Their life centred in Jerusalem and the Temple; but the synagogue had been retained as a permanent institution, and was a vital centre of non-sacrificial worship and study of the Scriptures. The presiding officials in the synagogues were the scribes, laymen whose business it was to interpret the Law, which reached its present form in the fourth century. This new Judaism bred the deep personal religion that characterises the Psalms; and if the general outlook was puritan rather than catholic, its institutions expressed at least desire of approach to God, and the unrealised hopes and ideals of the prophets were kept alive by a faithful remnant.   One of these, whose name is unknown, used an old story about the prophet Jonah, who had lived in the reign of Jeroboam II, to convey the truth of Israel's vocation as shown by Second-Isaiah.   Jonah, unwilling to be sent to the hated Assyrians at all, and still more angry when they show signs of grace, is the Chosen People, hugging her privileges and despising the Gentiles whom she was meant to enlighten.*

Meanwhile the days of Persian rule were drawing to a close.

* The cuneiform sign for Nineveh is a fish in a tank.   This may have suggested the story of Jonah and the Whale.

CHAPTER X

THE CHOSEN PEOPLE

(v) The Greek Period

THE Persian Empire founded by Cyrus extended westward into Asia Minor. There on the Aegean Coast at the outset of the fifth century the Persians came into conflict with the Greeks; and soon carried the war into the enemy's country. In 480, ten years after their great repulse at Marathon, the Persians returned by way of Thermopylae and burnt Athens.

These Greeks were originally a virile but unlettered tribe who called themselves Hellenes and lived on the banks of the Danube. While Abraham and his immediate descendants were living in Canaan the Greeks were pressing through the Balkan passes into the peninsula and islands, where they found in possession, especially in Crete, a mysterious people whom for lack of better knowledge we call the Aegeans. These people had an advanced civilisation derived partly from Egypt and partly from Mesopotamia, and possessed the art of writing in a form which so far baffles all attempts to read it. The Greeks conquered the Aegeans and adopted their civilisation. They began to commit their language to writing, but for this purpose they chose, not the Aegean but the Phoenician alphabet, of which the Hebrew was a variant. Some of the consonant sounds represented in this alphabet did not exist in Greek, so the Greeks used the superfluous symbols to represent the vowels which in Phoenician and Hebrew were not written at all.

By the time the conflict with Persia began, Greece had long been the home of the greatest art, literature, and philosophy ever known, but she had never become a world-power because the little states of which by her natural configuration she was composed were always fighting each other.* The one thing the Greeks did not understand was unity.

In the middle of the fourth century,—perhaps while R^{JP} was compiling the Pentateuch in Palestine,—a Macedonian Prince of the name of Philip, who had spent some years as a hostage in Greece and admired everything Greek except their disunion, managed on his return to make himself head of a league of Greek states, and also to secure the philosopher Aristotle as tutor for his young son Alexander. Having improved on the Greek art of war, Philip then asked the Greeks to avenge the sack of Athens, a hundred and fifty years before, by joining him in a campaign against the Persians. His preparations were almost complete when he was murdered at his daughter's wedding; and Alexander, aged nineteen, took on both the league and the campaign.

The story of Alexander the Great is one of the most amazing in history. In a few years he made himself master of the whole of the Persian Empire in western Asia and Egypt, and even got as far as India. His aim was to found a world-empire, Greek-speaking and Greek-thinking; and to this end wherever he went he founded Greek cities. The chief of these was his name-city, Alexandria, at the mouth of the Nile; and in it he planted a large colony of the Jews, for whom he had a strange respect, thus making a large and important increase in the extent of the Dispersion.

When Alexander died, at the age of thirty-three, leaving

---

* The Greek *language*, for the same geographic reason, consisted of a number of different dialects, that used in Attica, of which Athens was the capital, being the most highly developed. When Greeks from all states joined up in Alexander's army a common language was evolved on an Attic basis which became the so-called Hellenistic Greek of the Septuagint and, later, the New Testament.

no possible heir, his vast empire fell to his generals. Chief among them were Seleucus, who got Syria and Asia Minor, and Ptolemy, who got Egypt and Palestine. As all the successors of Ptolemy bore his name, the time during which the Jews were under their rule,—from 331 to 198 B.C. is known as the Ptolemaic period. After that they passed for nearly sixty years under the rule of the Seleucid kings of Syria.

The Greek influence which now for the first time poured in upon the Chosen People was two-sided. On the one hand there was Greek philosophy, that profoundest and wisest product of human thought, which carried with it a lofty view of the human soul and of moral duty. On the other side there was Greek irreligion and Greek immorality. The Gods of Olympus who had inspired the heyday of Greek art were at best non-moral, while at worst their cultus was made the occasion for every form of vice. A highly developed sense of natural beauty and the joy of living is a dangerous thing when there is no moral sense to control it; and as the representation of the human form in art had hitherto been forbidden to the Jews on account of its connection with idolatry, the things in which the Greeks most delighted had for the Jews all the charm of novelty. The Ptolemaic period was thus a time both of deadly peril and of great educational possibility.

Into the backwater of Palestine itself Greek influence surged like a spring tide; and the result was a cleavage and a crisis. Many apostatized; others, though remaining Jews in name, caught the Greek madness. At the head of this wordly party, carefully keeping in favour with their heathen rulers, were the high priests; but, as always, there was a faithful remnant: a party which clung fiercely to their faith and the Law and hated everything Greek.

With the Jews of the Dispersion in Alexandria the case was somewhat different. They were a respected and influential section of the population, and though apostasy and compromise were not lacking among them, many of the better Greeks frequented the synagogues and studied the Scriptures. By order of one of the Ptolemies a Greek translation was made of the latter, which from the tradition that it was the work of seventy scholars is known as the Septuagint. This is the version of the Scriptures most frequently quoted in the New Testament, and has peculiar value, partly as deriving from the unpointed Hebrew texts, now non-existent, and partly as being the first attempt to express Hebrew thought in the Greek language.

When good Jews met good Greeks in the liberal atmosphere of Alexandria, they were bound to try to effect some sort of synthesis between revelation and the best elements in pagan philosophy; and the fruit of this effort appears in the Book of Wisdom. 'The wise' were a class of teacher among the Chosen People which came to the fore after the Exile, when prophecy had waned. All the Wisdom books are based upon the Hebrews' certainty of God: their aim is to show how the facts of experience may be reconciled with His righteous governance, and to apply the principles of the Law and the Prophets to daily life. Most of them show some influence of foreign culture, but the author of the 'Wisdom of Solomon' seems actually to have known the works of several Greek philosophers at first hand, and combines some of their teaching with his own faith. Especially interesting is the way in which he represents the Divine Wisdom as the agent not only of creation but of all God's dealings with humanity. We have already seen a tendency to personify the attributes of God in Ezekiel's language about His Spirit or Breath, as the means by which Israel should be renewed. These personifications spring from transcendent monotheism *plus* the companion certainty that God is in close and constant touch with man. There is no thought as yet of distinction of persons in God. His Wisdom and later still His Word through whom He acts, though personified are not yet persons; and His Spirit is no more than His creative energy. But the soil is being prepared none the less for the revelation of the Trinity.

The transference of Palestine from Ptolemaic to Seleucid rule in 198 B.C. divided the Jews of the homeland into two camps, of Egyptian and Syrian sympathies respectively.

In 168 B.C. the Syrian King Antiochus Epiphanes, chagrined at his failure to annex Egypt and incensed against the Egyptian party in Palestine, determined to stamp out Judaism by persecution. He first issued an edict that the Jews should sacrifice to the gods or die; and then on 25th December of the same year,—the heathen festival of the Sun,—profaned the Temple at Jerusalem by sacrificing a sow to Zeus on the brazen altar.

His action caused the saving of the faith which it was calculated to destroy. In face of the prevailing apostasy and indifference one family,* a priest named Mattathias and his five sons, raised the standard of revolt; and fleeing to the wilderness rallied round them the *perūshîm* or pious, —the faithful remnant of the day. From the noblest of the five brothers, Judas Maccabaeus or the Hammer, who soon succeeded his father in the leadership, this is known as the Maccabaean Revolt, which before long merged into the War of Independence.

Within three years Judas had gained such victories over the Syrian armies that he was able on 25th December, 165, exactly three years after the profanation, to rededicate the Altar and the Temple, an event which was celebrated to the end of Jewish national history as the Feast of the Dedication.

Shortly after this the persecuting Antiochus died; but the war was carried on first with his son Antiochus Eupator and then with his nephew Demetrius, who should by rights have reigned before his uncle. At this juncture, Judas

* See table in appendix.

took the wise step of making a treaty with the then rising power of Rome for the protection of his people. Shortly afterwards he died in battle, and was succeeded by his youngest brother, Jonathan, who managed in a few years to make himself master of most of Palestine. But the ideals of the Maccabees had changed greatly since the beginning of the war. Mattathias and Judas fought and died for freedom to hold the faith of their fathers and to observe the Law; Jonathan and his successors sought political independence also, and were not over-particular how they got it. Thus it came about that Jonathan accepted the High-Priesthood from Demetrius' rival Alexander, because it gave him the leadership of his people, —a position which he skilfully maintained till his death.

Only one of the five sons of Mattathias now remained; and he, Simon, succeeded to his brother's office. Under him in 140 B.C. the political independence of the Jews was achieved and a peaceful rule established under the wing of ever-rising Rome.

The transference of the High-Priesthood from the direct Aaronic line to the branch line of the Maccabees seems at first sight unintelligible in view of the position enjoyed by the Aaronic High-Priesthood since the Return. But the Aaronic family had become hopelessly discredited with all patriotic Jews by reason of their time-serving attitude to their Greek rulers; moreover, since four years before the persecution, when Antiochus Epiphanes had intruded into the office one Menelaus, who was not of the priestly family at all, the legitimate High-Priesthood had been maintained only at the rival Temple of Leontopolis in Egypt, where many Palestinian Jews took refuge. The Maccabees were the saviours of their people and had proved their fitness to rule; they were at any rate of the priestly family, and Jonathan's appointment, though at the hands of a heathen, seemed right and obvious. There are even indications of some expectation of the Messiah from the tribe of Levi instead of that of Judah, so completely had the High Priest assumed the rôle of theocratic King.

The faith which flamed up in the Maccabaean revolt found literary expression in the form known as Apocalyptic. Apocalyptic, which means simply *that-which-reveals*, is prophecy cast in the form of symbolic or figurative visions, the material of which is derived partly from tradition and earlier prophecy and partly from things of common experience. Examples of it have already been noted in Ezekiel and Zechariah, but the first Apocalypse proper is the Book of Daniel, which reflects the persecution of Antiochus, from 168 to 165 B.C.; and the others, most of which are not in the Canon of Scripture, date from that time to about A.D. 100.

At the time when the Apocalypses began to appear the Prophetic Canon of the Old Testament was closed; and the Law was regarded as having taken the place of prophecy as the organ of revelation. Consequently a man who felt he had a message from God could not expect to gain a hearing for it unless he put it forth under the name of some known man of God, who had lived before the closing of the Canon. The Jewish Apocalypses are consequently all pseudonymous, bearing such names as Enoch, Moses, Isaiah and Abraham. This pseudonymity is not quite on a par with the ascription of all Law to Moses and all Psalms to David, but by the literary and historical standards of the time it was equally admissible.

The Apocalypses show great development of doctrine in several directions. In all of them the desperate circumstances from which they sprang exercise a strong influence. There is a great insistence on the nearness of the Day of the Lord, but that day is thought of as one of vengeance on the heathen oppressors of His people, not, as in the prophets as one of judgment for themselves whose approach called for moral and social reform. It is easy to condemn this as a less exalted view; but one should remember that the writer of Daniel had experienced the horrors so baldly stated in the seventy-ninth Psalm, and that the other Apocalyptists lived in times scarcely less terrible.

As with the prophets, the Day of the Lord is expected to usher in the Messianic Kingdom or era, but this is conceived as a heavenly kingdom that rises upon the ruins of the earthly. There is little thought of a personal Messiah, but when he appears he also is a heavenly rather than a human figure. In the Book of Jubilees he is described as a 'Son of Man'; and in Enoch he is 'Son of God,' a title already applied poetically to the expected Son of David, but now used with more transcendent meaning. This again is easy to understand in view of the times that gave it birth: for this world there was seemingly no hope save that it and the evil with it should be utterly destroyed, but faith in God as Dependable Reality could look beyond this world for the promised future, and cling to the belief, so often corroborated in history, that 'the darkest hour comes before the dawn.'

The same daring faith sees all history as the unfolding of the purpose of the One transcendent God Whom the Jews alone worship, and at the same time the longing of man to know God *near* fills the gap between his own little-ness and God's infinitude with an elaborate system of angelic intermediaries,* while all earthly conflicts are regarded as having their counterpart in the unseen world: Michael, the angelic prince of Israel, fights for them with the evil powers that rule the earth.

The many martyrdoms of the Maccabaean period led to wider ideas about the future life. Hitherto the Jews as a body had not progressed very far beyond the Baby-lonian notion of Sheol, a gloomy abode beneath the earth,

---

* The doctrine of angels, good and bad, owes a great deal to Persian influence. Ezekiel's later visions are mediated by an angel. Compare Daniel, and St. John in the Christian Apocalypse.

where souls had a shadowy existence remote from God. With the growth of the doctrine of the individual, however, some at any rate had come to hold that a man's fellowship with God was maintained and even strengthened after death; and now the conviction took form that those who died for their faith would be individually rewarded in the heavenly kingdom hereafter, as their enemies would be punished, in their bodies. Thus the problem of just reward and punishment is met by the doctrine of personal resurrection.

The home of the Apocalypses was Galilee, and the doctrines which they contained were popular chiefly among the common people. Official Judaism spurned them as unjustified accretions: hence the cleavage in later times between the popular leaders, the Pharisees, and the Sadducees 'who say that there is no resurrection.'

The developments of doctrine both in Alexandria and in Palestine outlined in this chapter continued beyond the Greek period up to and even after the time of Our Lord, but have been mentioned here in connection with the circumstances which first stimulated their growth.

CHAPTER XI

THE CHOSEN PEOPLE

(vi) The Shield and Yoke of Rome

THE Jews had succeeded in wresting their independence from the Seleucid kings largely because these were themselves menaced by the new power in the West, under whose protection Judas had wisely placed his cause.

The Roman people were the descendants of the Latins, a group of the Aryan tribes which had entered Italy through the passes of the Alps at about the same time that the Greeks entered the Balkan peninsula. In the middle of the eighth century B.C.,—the time of Amos and Hosea in Palestine,—the Latins in mid-Italy were conquered by the sea-roving, non-Aryan Etruscans, who came probably from the west of Asia Minor. Under the Etruscan kings the Latin settlement of Alba Longa on the Tiber became the city-kingdom of Rome and acquired a measure of civilisation while retaining its own language and tribal identity. After some two and a half centuries the Latins expelled their Etruscan rulers and established a Republic of their own.* By a series of intertribal wars Rome then attained a hegemony in Italy which was all the more secure because, unlike the great powers of the East, she made allies and not slaves of the peoples whom she conquered.

* c. A.D. 500. Horatius who kept the bridge is thus roughly contemporary with Malachi.

In the third century Rome came into conflict with Carthage, the powerful Phoenician trading centre in North Africa, over the trade in Sicily: and, thanks to the loyalty of her allies, emerged from the third and last of these Punic wars mistress* of the Western Mediterranean. She then turned her attention eastward to Macedonia, whither the Carthaginian general Hannibal had fled for aid after his defeat in Italy; and in 197, the year after Palestine passed to the Seleucids, the ancient realm of Alexander became vassal to Rome. Hannibal was by this time hand in glove with Antiochus the Great† so Rome had no choice but to attack the Seleucid Empire also. In 190 Antiochus was defeated on his own soil, and Asia Minor west of the Halys river became Roman territory. In 168 Egypt entered into voluntary vassalship to Rome in order to escape conquest by the fourth Antiochus, who, as we saw, relieved his feelings by persecuting the Jews.

The effect upon Rome herself of the annexation of so much of what had been Alexander's Empire was two-edged. She gained immensely in culture and wealth, and was herself conquered by the Greek language, which was henceforward the *lingua franca* of her dominions, though never to the exclusion of Latin in the West. But she lost, as Israel had lost under Solomon, only on a much larger scale, in the simplicity and purity of her social life. Her power grew without her virtue, and the administration of government both at home and in the provinces became utterly corrupt. A few years after the Jews had won their independence under her wing, Rome herself entered on a century of revolution and class war, in which one great leader after another,—Marius, Sulla, Pompey, Julius Caesar, Mark Antony,—held the reins of power. Finally

* The Romans called the Carthaginians *Poeni* or Phoenicians: whence Punic.

† Antiochus III, father of Antiochus IV (Epiphanes). See table in Appendix.

in 30 B.C. Octavian, the astute and worthy nephew of the great Julius, received from the Senate the titles of Augustus and Imperator as well as that of Caesar. The Roman Republic had become the Roman Empire, a great cosmopolitan unity which, in spite of its continued social corruption, was soon to be as remarkable for its political virtues as the Republic had been for its vices.

We must now return to the history of the Chosen People at the point where we left it in 140 B.C.

After the murder of Simon the Maccabee, his son John Hyrcanus succeeded to his office of Ethnarch and High-Priest. The reign of John Hyrcanus is remarkable for three things. He went to war with the Samaritans, whose territory lay like a wedge in the middle of his dominions, and overthrew both the rival sanctuary on Gerizim and the city of Shechem or Sychar at its foot. He invaded the territory of the Edomites or Idumaeans,—the traditional descendants of Esau,—in the south, and forced them to be circumcised and incorporated into the Jewish Church; and finally he broke with the patriotic and religious party and made alliance with the Hellenizers. As he also regained the territory of the two and a half tribes east of Jordan, his dominions at the time of his death in 107 B.C. were larger than those of any Jewish king since Solomon. His son Alexander Jannaeus maintained his father's policy; but under Alexander's widow Alexandra the popular Pharisaic party for a time regained power; and it is not surprising that this period was marked by a recrudescence of the older form of the Messianic hope,—that of an earthly kingdom under a descendant of David.

On the death of Alexandra, however, civil war at once broke out between her sons, Hyrcanus and Aristobulus. Hyrcanus the elder was a weakling, completely under the thumb of his adviser, Antipater the Idumaean, but Aristobulus was a person of parts. Finally both brothers appealed to Rome for arbitration, and were summoned before Pompey, then at the zenith of his power. Pompey gave judgment in favour of Hyrcanus and then besieged and took Jerusalem, where Aristobulus had taken refuge. It was on this occasion that Pompey, curious to know what manner of idol the Jews worshipped, insisted on entering the Holy of Holies, to the unspeakable horror of the Jews, and the equal surprise of himself, when he found it empty.

After this event in 63 B.C. Hyrcanus, though allowed to retain his titles, had greatly reduced territory and paid annual tribute to Rome. The days of Jewish independence were over.

For the next twenty-six years the descendants of John Hyrcanus strove each to further his own interests by gaining favour with the prevailing power at Rome. When Caesar defeated Pompey at Pharsalus, Antipater quickly won the victor's aid for the side of Hyrcanus. Antipater himself was poisoned soon after this, but his son Herod was equally adroit in winning the friendship of Antony after Caesar's murder. His client Hyrcanus having been taken prisoner, Herod got possession of the grandchildren of Aristobulus, a boy of the same name and a girl, Mariamne, whom he afterwards married. He took these children to Rome and, posing to Antony as the protector of the boy, won the title 'King of the Jews' *for himself*. With the help of a Roman army he then wrested his kingdom from the hands of the children's uncle, Antigonus. In this struggle, in the year 37, the Temple was wrecked; but in order to gain favour with his subjects Herod rebuilt it on a magnificent scale, and imported a member of the direct Aaronic family from Egypt to be its High-Priest. After his accession to power, Herod, who was jealous to to the point of madness, caused the murder of all the remaining Maccabees, including, ultimately, his own wife and her sons. He also took fearful vengeance upon the

Sadducees who had opposed him. When Antony fell before Octavian, Herod, prompt with his assurance of loyalty, was reinvested by him with the title 'King of the Jews.'

Herod the Great is the most pitiful figure in history. Ambitious and gifted, yet forever defeating his own ends, craving for love and meriting hatred, he is a type of the fallen race at its worst and neediest, the race that has turned aside from its path of progress towards God and finds itself trapped in a *cul-de-sac*, frustrated, unsatisfied, helpless. As he grew older he grew worse, and vented his insane cruelty without restraint on a people already demoralised by civil war, torn by party strife and sapped by heathen influence. Yet that people was the seed of Abraham who, twenty-one centuries before, had come to that country at the bidding of God, just at the time when two great groups of Aryan tribes from central Europe, the one of imaginative, the other of practical genius, were entering Greece and Italy respectively as unconscious instruments of the same Divine purpose. Things looked black enough outwardly, but for all that, or rather just because of it, the Bridge of which Abraham was the foundation was very nearly completed. History was converging on the faithful remnant, hidden like leaven in the lump of Herod's subjects. They were none of them conspicuous people, but they came from every section of the nation,—an old priest and his wife at Hebron, a couple of aged folk in Jerusalem, regular in attendance at the Temple, a few fisher-families on the Sea of Galilee, some shepherds on the Bethlehem hills, a peasant couple at Nazareth, descendants of David, who had a little daughter and an old kinsman who was a carpenter. These people held the faith in the One Holy God whose development we have tried to trace. *Truth* to them meant God revealing Himself in Self-consistent action. In spite of the desperate present they believed that He would again intervene in human history to put things right. There were many elements in this hope: some looked for an earthly, others for a heavenly Messiah; some saw His coming as glory for Israel only, others saw it also as a light for the Gentiles; some pictured the Kingdom as royal, others as priestly, having its one centre of worship in the Temple and consisting only of those who had been admitted to a new Covenant with God. All must have pondered the figure of the Suffering Servant, but none identified him with the Messiah.

In this alone all who hoped at all were agreed: they all looked for *God Himself* to act; for God in some way to rend the heavens and come down.

On a day, probably in March of the year we reckon as 7 B.C., the daughter of the Davidic family at Nazareth had a theophany. She learnt that God wanted her to be the mother of the Messiah, Son of David and Son of God, not by the agency of a human father but by the power of Holy Spirit.

Like her forefather Abraham, Mary was free and the future of the world hung upon her response. Also like him, she believed *in* God as dependable Reality, and therefore obeyed. '*And Mary said: Behold the handmaid of the Lord; be it unto me according to Thy word.*'

This is the second of the three sentences which might well be printed in gold.

Perhaps eighty years later, an old man who came from one of those good fisher-families in Galilee expressed what happened at that moment, in the light of his own experience of Mary's Son in these words: '*The Word was made Flesh and dwelt among us.*'

God had acted. He by Whom all things were made, in Whom they all consist, had, unknown to anyone save her whose obedience made it possible, Himself as man entered the created order. The Keystone of the Bridge was at last in being.

As S. John used the thought-forms of his day, so we may get help from those current in our own. Science has shown us that the universe is an organic unity; that the cosmic series, progressing from level to level in the direction of individuality which is the likeness of God, culminates in man; and that man alone of all creatures consciously reaches out beyond himself to find his satisfaction in God; but owing to the Fall fails perfectly to do so.

Each level of the series takes up into itself all lower levels under its own principle of unity, so that in man, the crown of the series, all creation is included. The Incarnation of the Word was thus a new creation, for by it humanity was taken up on to the level of God. The principle of unity in the Sacred Humanity is no mere human individuality but the Person of God the Word. The 'I,' the *Ego* in Jesus *is* Almighty God. By His taking of the Manhood into Himself the movement of creation towards God was re-established: the human race began again in a Second Adam.

The earthly life of the Incarnate Word and His rejection by His own people forms the subject of Chapters XIII to XVI. It remains here only to trace the history of the Chosen People up to the close of their national history and existence. With the passage of the faithful remnant of A.D. 29 into the new Chosen People, the Christian Church, the work of the old Israel was done. They lingered as a nation for some forty years, still offering their superseded sacrifices and looking vainly for the Messiah of their own imaginings, who would restore the Davidic Kingship and loose them from the Roman yoke. This hope led to fruitless rebellion, and in A.D. 71, after a terrible siege, Jerusalem and the Temple with it were destroyed by the Romans.

The seed of Abraham according to the flesh are a people still, to be found in every country of the world, yet calling none their own. And in every age they have been, as they are even now in Germany, like the Suffering Servant of their own prophecy, hated and persecuted of men.

"Behold the handmaid of the Lord"

H

CHAPTER XII

INTRODUCTION TO THE NEW TESTAMENT

HAVING run already on to New Testament ground at the close of the last chapter, we pause now to review the sources of the ensuing narrative. In point of date, the first books in the Christian Canon are the thirteen Epistles attributed to S. Paul, all of which were written between the years A.D. 49 and 64. Set as they are against the background of the Apostle's own oral teaching and of abundant tradition based on still living memory, some of which was later embodied in the written gospels, these letters do not narrate the life of Jesus, nor do they give a formulated scheme of Christian doctrine. Rather they show that doctrine being born of experience,—a thrilling process, somewhat obscured for us by the stately English that replaces the often colloquial but always vital Greek of the original. On the heels of the Pauline epistles in regard to time comes the little Gospel of S. Mark, followed within ten years by S. Matthew's—so-called, and S. Luke's with its sequel Acts. These three are known from their common view-point and plan as the Synoptic Gospels; but there is a great difference between the first-named and the other two. Mark was by ancient tradition interpreter to S. Peter, and all through his book there throbs like a held pedal on the organ Peter's retrospective penitence. 'So foolish was I and ignorant even as it were a beast before Thee,' he seems to say; and it is bluntly as uncomprehending beasts that Mark, echoing Peter, shows the apostolic band, leaving it to Luke in Acts to show the beauty into which their Master's faith in them developed them. Mark's story is in consequence like a home-made film. It has no polish,—his Greek is almost the worst in the Bible,—no touching-up; it is simply bald truth, terrible and lovely both at once. S. Luke and the author of the first gospel, on the other hand, are more like professional photographers, the former especially being an artist at his work. They do not originate, they edit. They tone down Mark's snapshots and set with them pictures from other sources. One of these sources, used by both, is the mysterious Q, so-called from the German *Quelle*, a source, which may well have been the original 'Sayings of Jesus' compiled by the Apostle Matthew. Each of these evangelists has also a special source of immense value, from which he derives, among other things, those beloved stories of Our Lord's infancy, full of angels and signs from heaven, that show Him as the fulfilment of all Old Testament prophecy; and it is with his record of these events,— quite naturally, since they occurred first,—that each begins.

The Fourth Gospel was probably written not very long after the later Synoptics, but it is separated from them by a difference greater than any difference of time. It cannot be doubted that S. John knew the Synoptics and designed to supplement them; what he gives us is not a snapshot or a finished photograph, but a portrait from life by a master hand. A modern writer has said that whereas Mark records what Jesus *did*, Matthew what He *said* and Luke what He *felt*, John tells you what He *intended*,—and, one might add, *Who He is*. For John, gathering for his purpose the treasures of Greek as well as of Hebrew thought, begins with the dogma of the Word Incarnate; and, as he proceeds, passes imperceptibly from recording what Jesus actually said to explaining in his own words what he now knows that Jesus meant. How should it be otherwise? Our Lord Himself promised that the Holy Spirit, when given, should bring His teaching to His friends' remembrance and enable them to understand it. It is in the nature of living things to grow, and the *ipsissima verba* of the Incarnate Word could hardly be an exception.

Leaving the fourfold gospel and passing over the other than Pauline epistles which, with the exception of II Peter, probably all belong to the sixties and seventies, we are left with one book in the New Testament which is the most disputed, the most difficult and the coping-stone of all. The Revelation or Apocalypse of John has close affinities with the Fourth Gospel, though it differs from it greatly in style; so it is quite permissible for people who do not want to go into critical questions to regard the visions as those of John the Evangelist, even if someone else, perhaps a disciple of the same name, wrote them down. The book, which in its present form at any rate dates from the Domitian persecution in A.D. 95, has the form of the Jewish apocalypses and, like them, aims at sustaining faith and hope in a desperate present. But just as its imagery is to a great extent borrowed not from the apocalyptists but from the prophets who preceded them, so do its vision and purpose go far beyond the present for which it was written. In the Apocalypse you see things whole: you see that the conflict between good and evil is age-long but *not* eternal: you see the working out of God's purpose in creation and redemption right up to its consummation in the *end* of evil and 'all things new.' We may be baffled by the Apocalypse, but we could not possibly do without it!

CHAPTER XIII

THE INCARNATE LIFE ON EARTH

(i) The Preparation

THE obvious thing to do now is to continue the narrative from the point reached at the end of Chapter XI,—the supreme yet secret moment of the Incarnation. That is how three evangelists approach the story of Jesus' later life, and from that standpoint we also normally view it. Approaching by the avenue of Bethlehem and Nazareth, we say of Jesus in His Ministry and Passion: 'This is God Incarnate, the Virgin-born'; and the instinct of reverence makes us represent Him in pictures as adorned with a visible halo or at least with so distinctive a dress as leaves no doubt which figure in the group is He. But this method of approach ignores the fact that that which was first in order of time in the Incarnate Life was last in order of apprehension; and it does less than justice to the complete-ness of the Divine Self-emptying. The contemporaries of Jesus did not say 'This is God' or 'This is the Virgin-born' or even 'This is the Christ.' At best they called Him 'the carpenter, the son of Joseph'; at worst, 'son of Mary,'* an echo from the troubled days before His birth when Mary had had to maintain her belief in God and in her own unique vocation all alone, for even Joseph was minded to put her away privily. And right at the end it was necessary for Judas to give the traitorous kiss in order to show the Temple guard which among twelve was Jesus. So for those who want to trace the experience of the first believers,—the experience of which was born belief in

* To call a Jew the son of his mother was to imply that he was illegitimate.

Him as both Christ and God *before* His Virgin-birth was known, the safest guide is the Gospel of St. Mark.

'Gospel' is S. Mark's own name for his book, and it may be said to be his own invention. For the noun *evangelion* in Hellenistic Greek did not mean 'good news' but only the reward given to someone who brought it. The verb *evangelizein*, however, had been used in the Septuagint to translate the Hebrew *bāsar*, which means to thrill or give joy by means of good news, particularly those of the birth of a child or of victory in battle. *In this sense* Mark uses the noun. He has no Infancy narrative and his Resurrection chapter breaks off, scarcely begun, in the middle of a sentence; yet the title of his book contains it all,—from the glad tidings of the birth at Bethlehem to those yet gladder of the Easter victory,—the Good News that *is* Jesus.

'*Beginning of the Good News of Jesus Christ.*

Just as it is written in (Isaiah) the prophet,

'Behold I am sending My Messenger before thy
face,
The which shall build thy road;
Voice of a crier in the desert:
Prepare ye the road of Jahveh,
Straight make ye His paths,'

JOHN CAME, the baptiser, in the desert, proclaiming baptism of repentance unto forgiveness of sins.'

The appearance of the Forerunner *was* for his contemporaries the beginning of the Good News,—the first they heard of it, stop-press from heaven. John, appearing from nowhere, for they did not know the story of his birth, told them that God was going to *act*, to show Himself true, as prophets and apocalyptists had foretold, by establishing at last His Kingdom. But the New Kingdom carried with it a New Covenant; and in the ministry of John, the New peeps already from the Old like a seedling from the soil. The Jews believed that their ancestors had been baptised before their admission to the Covenant at Sinai; and in later times baptism was used not only for the cleansing of those who had contracted Levitical defilement, but also in the admission of proselytes to Covenant relationship. John's baptism was therefore more than a token of forgiveness following an act of repentance or 'change-of-mind':* it was a sign that those who received it were preparing to be admitted to the New Covenant and Kingdom.

But who and where was the King?

Unlike the apocalyptists, John put the Person through whom the new age was to be inaugurated in the forefront of his message: yet he himself was ignorant of that Person's identity. The Forerunner, busy with his work of making ready, may not look behind him to see who it is that cometh after. Nevertheless the moment comes when the Comer catches up the Forerunner and they stand at last face to face.

That moment was the Baptism of Jesus.

'In those days came Jesus from Nazareth of Galilee and was baptised in Jordan,—literally *into*, implying immersion, —by John.' Thus Mark introduces the Comer as he introduced the Forerunner, without a word as to His earlier history. And truly Jesus also must have seemed to come literally from nowhere. Messianic expectation there was indeed, but it certainly was not focussed on Nazareth. Those who watched the building of Solomon's Temple never saw the great stones till they were ready to go into place, for they were shaped in the quarries. So John and Jesus, stone and Keystone of the Bridge, were prepared for thirty years, one in his desert, the Other in His home, and the eyes of those who looked for redemption in Israel turned to neither.

* The literal meaning of the Greek *metanoia*.

The Baptism of Our Lord, called anciently His Epiphany or Manifestation, is a great mystery, but certain points are clear. It was not a public event,—the crowds which had previously been baptised had gone away,—but a private revelation to the two. To John it was the climax of his vocation, the vision of the Dawn that bade the daystar fade: to Jesus it was the unveiling of what His vocation meant.

'*Thou art My Son the Beloved.*' 'Son of God' was a Messianic title; the adjective *agapētos*, here rendered 'beloved' is used in the Septuagint interchangeably with *monogenēs*, sole-begotten, to translate the Hebrew *yāḥîdh* which, coming from a root meaning to be united, to be one, has the twin senses of only and most dear. Its addition to 'My Son' implies therefore that the relationship of Jesus to God was in some sense unique. The phrase, 'In Thee I am well pleased,' together with the ensuing gift of Holy Spirit, echoes the passage in the Servant Song, 'My chosen in whom my soul delighteth, I have put my spirit upon him.' Thus Jesus learnt that He was to be *both Christ and Suffering Servant.*

'*And straightway the Spirit driveth Him forth into the wilderness, and He was in the wilderness forty days tempted of Satan.*'

Our minds shrink from contemplating the mystery of Our Lord's Temptation; and by the same instinct that makes us give Him a visible halo in pictures, we tend always to minimise its terrible, adorable reality. Yet there it is, an integral part of the gospel. St. Mark records bluntly the bare fact; the other synoptists, following Q, describe its threefold form. If Q was the original St. Matthew, we have probably got the story just as that apostle had it from the Lord Himself. In any case it *must* have come ultimately from Him; and its form, be it literal or allegorical, is that into which He put it, and the only one in which we could understand even the

outermost fringes of the mystery. What does it mean?
It means that the Incarnate Word, the Second Adam,
met the author of evil in single combat; and, just because
He resisted to the end, experienced *the full range* of his
seductive power. He was, to use a Jewish expression,
tempted from Aleph to Tau,* or, as we say, from A to Z,
so that there was absolutely no temptation left outside
His experience. And in trying thus to re-enact in the
Judaean wilderness the tragedy of Eden, the devil, with
the Second Adam as with the first, laid siege to just that
trinity of virtues which constitute man's right relationship
to God,—the faith and love and obedience which *are*
religion. 'If you are the Son of God as you have just
been told, use the miraculous powers you have just received to supply your own needs; command allegiance
by making a sensation; *take a short cut* to your goal.'

How steep, how cruelly blocked with thorny thicket
through its long disuse was the straight path up the mountain then! How hard to maintain that fundamental
trinity of virtues! But Jesus, true Man, staying Himself
upon revealed truth, held on; and at length the devil
departed from Him *for a season*.

Picture Jesus as He returns from the wilderness to
begin His public ministry, New Man Whose mission is
to make all things new. The Hebrew word for blessed
or happy† comes from a root meaning *to go straight forward*,
and thus counters the idea of sin, which means to go
crookedly. Was there ever anybody so happy as Jesus,
rejoicing as a giant to run His course?

---

* The first and last letters of the Hebrew alphabet, as Alpha and
Omega are of the Greek. It is worth noting that the Hebrew noun
'emeth, truth, referred to on p. 10, consists of three consonants, āleph,
mēm, tau,—the first, middle and last,—all-inclusive.

† as e.g. in Ps. i. 1, and cxix. 1. The word there is actually a
noun: 'O the happinesses of . . .'' Cp. its Greek equivalent *makarios*
in the Beatitudes.

CHAPTER XIV

THE INCARNATE LIFE ON EARTH

(ii) The Public Years

THE impression left on the minds of most people by the narratives of the Ministry is rather like the view you get by looking down a kaleidoscope. Miracles of healing and exorcism, miracles over nature, teaching in parable or otherwise to the many or the few, in which, elusive and paradoxical, the Kingdom of Heaven seems ever the central subject, glimpses of Our Lord's inner life as He prays alone on the mountain, individual contacts of Himself with others, scenes in street or by lakeside, in synagogue or in temple courts, pictures of His friends and of His enemies,—such are the pieces, each a jewel indeed, which shift ceaselessly beneath the eye, yet seem never to form a stable or intelligible pattern. The difficulty of seeing the Wood for the Trees is greater in the Gospels than anywhere; and in a sense it must always be so, just because what is there depicted is infinite and inexhaustible: the Wood is too big for human eye to see it all at once, and, as S. Augustine was once forcibly reminded, you cannot put the ocean into a teacup.

Nevertheless one can to some extent get inside the story by putting oneself in the place of those who took part in it,—those to whom, when Christmas was unknown and Easter had not happened, Jesus the Carpenter came from Nazareth of Galilee preaching the Good News of God. Suppose that it had happened in twentieth-century England, and He had come as a motor-mechanic from Birmingham.

The Pioneer of the untrodden highway came to the natives of the side-track, the prisoners in the cul-de-sac, first of all *as one of themselves*. But what He showed them was the perfection of human nature in its earthly state, and this was something entirely *new* that had never been seen before, and as such it was also the revelation to them of the character of God, no longer partial and fragmentary as under the old dispensation but *complete*. Mankind as a whole had been created to express God, to reflect Him as the lake reflects the scene above it. But whereas each human person was but as a single drop of water, reflecting a little bit, Jesus was *the whole lake*. In Him, Who was not *a* man but Man, was revealed 'all the fulness of the Godhead bodily.' And the poor sinful people among whom He lived were self-judged by their reaction to that supremely new revelation; like bottles receiving new wine they had either to stretch God knows how wide to hold it—or burst. The Light shone in the darkness and the darkness could neither understand it nor put it out.* It was not labelled as Light, so everything depended upon the individual's capacity for recognising the real thing when it was presented to him in the most unexpected forms and places.

We may be able to get a clearer view of what happened during the Ministry if we try to analyse the content of His perfection along the lines indicated in Chapter III. We saw there that man, and in a lesser degree all creation, resembles God in being at once individual, social and creative, diverse and yet one. Jesus is Absolute Individuality Incarnate: He alone is completely individual. For this reason He is paradoxical, because a paradox is contradiction yet completion, and the reconciling of opposites is essential to true completeness. For this reason also every race as well as every individual now finds

* Both these meanings are covered by 'comprehended it not' in Jn. 1[5].

in Him their ideal: He is universal Man Who includes them all; and for this same reason His friends at the time found Him difficult and His enemies impossible, because their ideas of perfection were at best relative and partial, while His standard of values was absolute and complete.

Jesus as Man is also socially perfect, both in relation to God and to His fellow-men. His Human life in regard to His heavenly Father is like that of one of those modern ships that are guided from the shore by a beam of light: it has no independent steering-gear, it just goes straight forward as the beam directs. His life is utterly simple, because only one thing matters and that is the will of God which He is always doing, His faith and love and obedience towards God never falter under all the hard conditions imposed by the fallenness of this world. His prayer is His life, and He alone in this dislocated scene is completely single-minded and at rest.

The relation of Jesus to His fellow-men can be summed up in two words: faith and love. Knowing them for what they are, He yet loves and believes in them as though they were already all that they are meant to be. And it is just that believing love of Jesus to men which is creative; that it is which, like the Breath from the four winds in the Valley of Dry Bones, brings Peter out of Simon and the apostle of love out of the son of thunder. It acts like sunshine on the buried seed, generating in those who respond to it faith and love and obedience towards Himself *like that* which He Himself renders to the Father. See how He stresses these things,—the three that are one,— in His teaching. Faith comes first, not a vague intellectual abstraction, but confidence in a known Person's utter dependability. 'Ye believe in God: believe also in Me.' (Imagine hearing that from a local carpenter.) 'Have ye yet not faith?' He asks wistfully, as though surprised that they found so hard to come by that which was for Himself the tissue of life. And always the one thing that really thwarts Him is *apistia*, unfaith, or as Wycliffe translates it, unbelievefulness. Nor is He less insistent on love, love to God and man, on which hangs all the Law and the prophets, and the obedience which follows from it: 'If ye love Me, ye will keep My sayings: ye are My friends if ye *do* whatsoever I command you.'

The creative energy of Jesus begins with individuals and of them forms a social unit, which is the extensive agent of the same power. S. Paul later on calls it His Body, because it shares His life and is His means of expression,—the New Humanity extended; but in Our Lord's own teaching it appears first and most often as the Kingdom of Heaven or of God, the mysterious new Kingdom that already is and yet is still to be. This Kingdom is contrasted with the old, already existing kingdom of this world; *and there is no other*. Men have got to belong to one or the other; indeed since the one is already in possession and the other but just beginning, the members of the new have to be won, rescued, from the tyranny of the old.

Just as in the Old Testament the Songs of the Suffering Servant, embedded in Second-Isaiah, stand almost alone as showing *how* redemption is to be effected, so there is one little bit of Our Lord's teaching, hidden in the Gospels like treasure in the field, which explains *how* the old kingdom is to be destroyed and the New set up. It is not usually accounted a parable; rather it is a drama—dare we say a comedy?—with two chief characters and no words, the sort that small children love to act. First appears a Strong Man, armed to the teeth and living in a fortified palace full of goods. The 'goods' include all the wretched, groaning captives whom the Lord of the House has taken and keeps there by means of his weapons. 'Goods' is a good name for them, for it is all they are, poor stunted personalities living in constant fear of those death-dealing spears and swords, and with no chance of escape or development. The Strong Man swaggers about the stage alone for a bit, so that you may take him well in; and then there walks quietly on Another, *unarmed*. You shrink in horror,—what chance has he against this tyrant? —but the new-comer goes straight up to the Strong One and takes his sword and his spear and all his weapons wherein he trusted from him. With them he defeats him, the Strong is bound by the Stronger than he, and the captives are loosed. There is a new Lord of the House* of humanity, the Same Who by His human birth at Bethlehem† had already rededicated it to God, in His own Person.

It is the same lesson as the Suffering Servant, but the other side of the picture. The weapons of the Evil One are all the consequence of sin which culminate in physical death. With them he keeps the human race in subjection and prevents its development according to God's intention. The Servant and the Stronger than the Strong are one; but whereas the Songs show you the reality and terribleness of the sufferings by which He saves, the Gospel shows you the reality of His joy in doing it. The one is read on Good Friday; the other ought to be read on Easter Day. It shows you that the whole idea of redemption *proceeds from that in God to which our humour corresponds*. We have not got a special word for it and we are afraid to use the ordinary ones lest they should sound irreverent. Yet the great Latin hymns of the Passion fearlessly express this idea,‡ and the drama of the Strong and the Stronger, like the story of David and Goliath, *is* gloriously and divinely humorous. The Strong is beaten *with his own weapons:* evil is made *to destroy itself.*

* The probable meaning of the Greek *Beelzeboul*, which by assimilation to the name in 2 K. 1², ⁶ appears in Latin MSS. and in our versions as Beelzebub.

† Traditionally on the very day of the Temple's rededication after Antiochus' pollution. See p. 85.

‡ See, e.g. *Pange Lingua*, English Hymnal, 95, verse 3.

This is the secret of redemption and of life. Who but Love, Eternal and Infinite, could have thought of it and laughed as He did so?

About six months before the end, the jewels in the kaleidoscope steady a little; and three events, occurring within one week, stand out clearly.

The first of these, the Feeding of the Five Thousand, is parable as well as miracle,—parable of the Lord's recreative mission to the starving world and of His intention to mediate His life by the hands of chosen men. Our word 'Lord' means bread-giver; and according to the Fourth Gospel this miracle, which took place on a Thursday, was followed on the next Sabbath by the discourse in which He spoke of Himself as the Living Bread come down from heaven for the life of the world,—strange words that at the time alienated many of His friends.

The next incident is S. Peter's confession. It is always rather difficult to realise that neither the preaching of the Baptist nor the course of the Ministry itself had brought any widespread conviction of Our Lord's Messiahship. When Peter, answering that epoch-making question near Caesarea Philippi, said 'Thou art the Christ,' he was expressing for the first time a faith that had cost the apostles hard travail of experience to bring forth. Even up to that time,—and how much more later!—Jesus was so different from the hero of popular expectation, so upsetting to their preconceived ideas and accepted standards and in such ill-odour with their religious leaders, that faith in His Messiahship, however limited in its conception, was a real achievement. It was a foundation; and on it He promptly built. 'The Son of Man must suffer . . . and be rejected . . . and be killed . . . ' Peter did not listen to the last bit, 'and after three days rise,' he was too much scandalised by the first. What *could* you do with such a leader, Who spoke of His rejection and death the moment after you had called Him Christ? It was preposterous. 'Be it far from Thee, Lord.' How pitiful is Peter, foolish and ignorant: how pitiful too is the loneliness of Jesus, breaking to His apostles the news of His Servant-Christhood,—that which was the very heart and centre of the Good News, really,—and having it thus received! But He goes, as ever, straight forward. Calling the crowd, He tells them that not for Himself only but for every human soul the way of the cross is the way of life, *and there is no other.*

③ The third event is the Transfiguration. Only the three, the inner circle of the apostles, saw it; and only in retrospect did any of them understand it. How could it have been otherwise? For what they saw was that which none had ever seen, of which none had ever dreamt,—the final, fulfilled perfection of humanity. To that by act of will the Second Adam passed: from that by act of will he returned to His earthly state. Why? As sinless Man, death was for Him no necessity: no abrupt change, no chrysalis stage need figure in His life-story, Who both could and did pass thus gently to His glory. But love overrides nature. The Servant-Christ *willed* to die that He might make His soul an offering for many. Only through death would He pass finally to His glory. We might well write below our Transfiguration pictures His own words: 'No man taketh My life from Me; I lay it down of Myself: I have power to lay it down and I have power to take it again.'

S. Luke adds a little bit to this story which the other evangelists have not got. He says that what Jesus and Moses and Elijah were talking about was 'the exodus that He should accomplish at Jerusalem.' Thus the Transfiguration appears as the porch to the Passion,— the actual entrance on the Great Deliverance.

So from the mountain, when they came down, Jesus 'set His face steadfastly to go up to Jerusalem.' Nor were

He and His the only travellers on the road. The crowds
were assembling for the Passover, preparing to commemo-
rate once again Israel's deliverance from Egypt by the
blood of the lamb and by the Act of God. It was the
Passover crowds which, in a sudden burst of enthusiasm
cried to Jesus as He entered the city, 'Hosanna to the Son
of David.' 'Hosanna' means *Save Now*.

That was exactly what He was going to do.

"How am I straitened till all be accomplished"

CHAPTER XV

THE INCARNATE LIFE ON EARTH

(iii) The Passion

THE Passion of Our Lord took place by divine arrangement at the Feast of the Passover.

It is uncertain whether the lambs were sacrificed at the actual time of His death or on the previous day, but that does not really matter. The fulfilment of type is perfect either way; and as long as we do not know which is right, we are free to enjoy both. The point to grasp is that those who witnessed and took part in the Passion, and who subsequently were the first Christian believers, experienced those events *in the setting* of the story of the Great Deliverance and of its commemoration. The Passover therefore provided them with the clue for understanding what the Passion meant.

Yet the Passover did not stand alone. Behind and around it lay all the Old Testament revelation of God as a God of action upon Whom His people can depend,— all that was summed up in the Hebrew conception of His truth, and demonstrated not only in the Exodus but throughout their history. And beyond the Passover lay the Day of Atonement, the highest human expression of the idea of sacrifice, of apology in symbol, by its very repetition self-confessed inadequate, yet serving to keep alive the sense of need and so to prepare for its satisfaction. All this was to the witnesses of the Passion utterly familiar. They had drunk it in with their mothers' milk; they could not remember a time when they had not known it.

On this foundation therefore, firm and solid as the ground at Bethel, God reared, ladder-like, the mystery of redemption, because when you want to teach you must of necessity begin with what your pupils know already: the

Birthplace } Borrowed.
Upper room }

tower that is to reach to heaven cannot be begun at the second storey. This does not mean of course that those people understood the Passion *at the time* in the light of their previous knowledge: on the contrary Holy Week was for them a furnace in which all the hopes which they had centred on Jesus were slowly burnt alive; nor could they then foresee that from those ashes would rise a phoenix of reality beyond all imagining. Only in retrospect did the Old Testament stand like a ring of mirrors round that week, both reflecting its events and itself illuminated by them. It is worth an effort, therefore, for us Gentiles whose experience begins with the commemoration of the Passion, viewed inevitably in the light of its sequel, to put ourselves back into the place of our first fathers in the Faith, and with them to follow Our Lord by His Cross and Passion to the totally unexpected glory of His Resurrection.

Let us begin with Thursday evening. The Lord had previously told the apostles to prepare the room,—borrowed, like His birthplace—where He might eat the Passover with them. The Synoptists take it that the supper on that night was the real Paschal Supper, following the sacrifice of the lambs in the afternoon. If this was so, Our Lord as head of the quasi-family must Himself have slain the lamb whose type He was within twenty-four hours to fulfil; and its body must have been actually on the table at the meal. The Fourth Gospel, however, says that Friday was the first day of the Feast, in which case Our Lord's death on the cross synchronised with the sacrifice of the lambs in the Temple, and the supper on the previous night was not the Paschal Supper but the *Kiddùsh*, a solemn meal of preparation for the Feast, followed by an appropriate sermon, which on this occasion was the discourse in chapters 14 to 17. But in either case it seems pretty clear that it was the ritual of the Paschal Supper which the Lord followed. If it was the wrong night, the apostles must have been amazed; but did not His every action that night fill them with stupefied and grieved amazement?

The Self-giving of Jesus at the Last Supper was effected in the threefold act of the Feetwashing, the Thanksgiving and the Command to eat His Body and to drink His Blood, presented to them under the separate forms of bread and of wine, and, further, themselves to do subsequently what He then did in remembrance of Him.

The condescension of the Feetwashing overwhelms us, as it did poor Peter; and we tend in consequence to view it rather as an isolated act than as what it really is,—a revelation of the *eternal* Servanthood of God, just as the Incarnation of the Word as a working-man is not a temporary dressing-up but a revelation of God in His eternal character of Worker. Service and Work are essential in God, active in the depths of His own triune Being or ever creation was, so that the form of a servant and of a working-man was the only congruous human form the Word could have taken; the element of suffering which is the result of the Fall alone being accidental. And since it is Love that ever serves and works, the virtuous circle comes round again to its beginning; and here in the Upper Room the Love of God which called man into being is manifested in his active service.

The Thanksgiving was a great deal more than merely saying grace over the bread and wine. Just as other people's minds were occupied at that time chiefly with the historic Exodus then being commemorated, Our Lord's was all on the divine Exodus which He was even then accomplishing. To thank God for anything is to recognise that it comes from Him and so to unlock its resources as a channel of blessing; and what Jesus gave thanks for in the same night in which He was betrayed was *His Passion,* all that armoury of weapons which He was wresting from the hand of Satan. In the crucible of love they are transmuted: by this willing, thankful receiving of them He makes *Himself*, betrayed, deserted, denied, hated, mocked, scourged, crucified, dead and buried, the supreme channel of blessing from God to man.

That He was a victim, the manner and the context of His gift plainly declared. The apostles were expecting either then or the next evening to eat the flesh of the sacrificial lamb which united them to God and to each other: it must have been obvious even at the time that the Lord was in some sense *substituting Himself* for the expected food. But it is hard to realise the shock to Jewish ears when He said of the Cup: 'This is My Blood of the New Covenant: *drink* ye of it.' It was indeed of the essence of a covenant that it should be sealed with the blood of sacrifice; and some notion of the Messianic Kingdom and of the New Covenant that went with it,—both seeming then so hopelessly remote,—must have been called up by the words. But such blood was only sprinkled; the Jews were expressly forbidden to drink blood or to eat meat containing blood *because the life is in it*. Exactly so. Peter and Andrew, James and John and all the rest of you now so pained and mystified, be not unbelieving. You have been brought up to eschew the blood of animals because theirs is a life on a lower plane than your own. What you are now bidden to drink is the Blood of the Incarnate Word, which by anticipation He is already pouring out in sacrifice for the sins of the whole universe. Through earthly flesh and blood you, like the rest of us, have received the tainted nature of the first Adam: by the same agency in its final and fulfilled perfection the Second Adam gives you now *His* life, the life that lifts man at last beyond himself into his home in God, thus consummating creation. And they *did* receive it. Then and there the New Covenant was inaugurated, the New Humanity, hitherto embodied in the sole Person of Jesus, was extended to them, though they knew it not, and were feeling wholly perplexed and miserable; for the merciful wisdom of God has made the towering mystery of communion entirely independent of our feelings.

Now follow those First Communicants through the waking nightmare that ensues. The earthly life-story of the Incarnate Word, the Way of Holiness, is a straight course up the mountain. He started at the very bottom,—the Aleph of conception; and now He has almost reached the top, and that is Tau, the Cross.* Here the thicket is densest, most wounding, most blinding: it is the last lap of the race, the last round of the duel between the Stronger and the Strong, and to all appearances the Strong has got the best of it. All that the eleven can see is *failure*. For as at the outset the mystery of redemption was hidden in silence, so now its climax is hidden in noise,—malice of enemies, lies of false witnesses, clamours of 'Crucify' and Satanic 'Ifs' hurled at the Crucified through human lips; and so great is the fury of the tempest over the abyss that nobody sees that the Keystone is quietly settling into its place *and finishing the Bridge*. The eleven are *in* Jesus through it all,—have they not drunk His Blood?—and their suffering is a thousandfold enhanced by their personal failure at the crisis. There is nothing left in them but *need* of Him Whom they have failed, Who has been taken from them and Whom they can never hope to see again. Self-sufficiency is dead, and they are just an emptiness. So there is room in them at last for His 'free bounty,'† but of course they do not yet realise that.

At the very top of the mountain there is just one foot-space of open ground. On that the Redeemer stands for one moment before He leaves the mountain for the higher world to which it has brought Him. On that He speaks the Sixth Word from the Cross, the golden *Tetelestai*.§

* The name of this letter means a sign or cross and its ancient form was × or +.

† The real meaning of *charis*, grace.

§ See pp. 34 and 95 for the two earlier golden words.

We miss the point of that in our translation, and even the Latin *'consummatum est'* does not quite get it. It is the Greek Perfect, which is used only of past action, *the results of which are still going on*. When a smith says of a sword-blade, 'It is finished,' he means that it is now ready for use. So with His Father's business, the Atonement. In this Word Jesus points to the Bridge of which He is Himself the Keystone newly placed, and says to the whole human race, 'This is the Way: walk ye in it.'

How happy is the death of Jesus! How happy beyond all thought His epiphany in Paradise! Virgil has pictured the disembodied souls of men crowding like dead leaves on the shore of Styx and begging Charon to ferry them over; but the boat is small and few find place. Here is a Charon Whose boat and heart are big enough to take them all. To the spirits in prison, to Adam, Abraham, David, Alexander, Julius Caesar, and all the myriads, known and unknown, who since the race began have experienced death and found no issue from it, comes the Second Adam, discarnate like themselves, with tidings that *the door is open*. 'When Thou hadst overcome the sharpness of death, Thou didst open the Kingdom of Heaven to all believers.' The New Covenant in His Blood looks back as well as forwards: the New Humanity shall be eventually coextensive with the old.

When Jesus died, the veil of the Temple was rent in twain from the top to the bottom. It is S. Mark who records that and one wonders what S. Peter thought when he first heard of it. The veil of the Temple was the curtain that separated the Holy Place from the Holy of Holies, the innermost sanctuary of God. According to tradition it had needed renewal shortly before Our Lord's birth and His mother had been chosen to spin the 'true purple' for it. Nobody ever went through the veil except the High Priest on the Day of Atonement, and then he went in alone, clad in garments of humiliation and bearing, together with incense, the blood of victims previously slain as sin-offerings. He did not stay there, nor did he make a way through for other people. He came out again, dismissed the scape-goat, the sin-bearer, and then, having changed into the golden garments proper to his office, reappeared before the expectant people, having ratified their covenant-relationship with God *for one year*. Meanwhile the veil hung dark across the empty sanctuary; no eye could pierce it, no representative of man pleaded with God beyond it. Next year a new High Priest would be in office, and the same thing would be done all over again. But at the moment of Jesus' death the veil was *rent* because to That which the Holy of Holies symbolised He, Himself scape-goat, sin-offering and priest, had made *a way through*. Moreover His sin-offering, being adequate since Himself is sinless, had never to be repeated; and we are still waiting for our High Priest to re-appear in the glorious raiment of His office.

You sometimes meet in fairy-tales with a creature conveniently possessed of three heads, which if it lose two of them can carry on with the third till the others have grown. So it is with the trinity of virtues, faith and love and obedience. When Jesus died, the faith of His friends in Him was cut off, and obedience went out of action because there was nothing to obey. But love persisted, and tided them over till on Easter Day faith and obedience rose with their Object. Of course they had only a dead Jesus to Whom to show their love, but that was better than nothing: so two men, who had never before dared openly show Him friendship, took His body down and buried it after the Jewish fashion. That is to say, the tomb was a cave hewn out of rock with a ledge for the body and a round stone to block the door. There was no coffin, but the Body was wrapped from shoulders to feet in long wide bandages with spices,—to which pot-pourri is perhaps the nearest thing in our experience,—sprinkled between the folds: a separate cloth went round the Head. It was done in a hurry, because the Sabbath was approaching, which left a further chance for others who loved Him, when the Sabbath was over, to go and do a little more— always supposing that they could get in. But it was only His Body. He was dead, and the light of life had gone out with Him. They did not realise that it had only gone just round the corner into Paradise. Nor did any, apparently, remember for their comfort that it is always the darkest hour that comes before the dawn.

CHAPTER XVI

THE INCARNATE LIFE ON EARTH

(iv) The Resurrection and Ascension

SUNDAY morning early, while it is yet dark.

The sleepless hours of that interminable Sabbath are over at last, and the women, broken and ravaged by their fellowship in the Passion, approach the tomb. 'And when they looked, they saw that the stone was rolled away, for it was very great.' *Alleluia*, adds the Easter antiphon, as much as to say, of course it was, God being what He is. And going in, they found the Body gone. The Resurrection had already happened, and neither they nor any other witnessed it. Thus the mystery of the Incarnation was consummated even more hiddenly than it had begun: Mary had opened the door of creation for the Word to enter; but no human hand opened the tomb, nor was it necessary that it should be opened, except to show that it was empty. The Resurrection was pure Act of God, the Truth's supreme Self-vindication.

S. Mark takes us as far as the terrified amazement of the women; and then he stops.* It is usual to talk about

---

* 'For they were afraid—' Afraid of what? The word translated 'for' follows the verb in Greek and is one that can in no case come at the end of a sentence.

the 'lost ending' of S. Mark, the supposition being that the end of the roll was torn off, and the present conclusion added in the next century by some prosaic soul who thought it untidy to stop in the middle of a sentence. But there is not a particle of evidence that S. Mark's gospel ever did end. It is at least as likely that he left off simply because he could not go on. He himself experienced Easter Day, and knew the fact and perhaps the details,—if Peter ever brought himself to tell them,—of the risen Lord's first meeting with the apostle who had denied Him. There are limits to what can be put into words, especially written words; and wise men do not try to force them.

It seems that the women did not all react alike to the experience at the tomb. All were frightened and amazed at first, all missed the lovely laughter in the angel's intimation that a tomb was the wrong place to seek the living Lord. But whereas to some as they sped back in the broadening sunrise,—and it was the same sun that rose this morning—the light of faith also began to dawn, to Mary Magdalen this new turn of events was only the final drop in her cup of woe. It was not the angel's message that she took to Peter and John, but her own. 'They have taken away my Lord, and I know not where they have laid Him.'

To the tomb forthwith ran Peter and John, followed, it would seem, by Mary Magdalen. The thing that struck the apostles when they reached the tomb was the grave-clothes. John, arriving first, glanced at them* through the doorway: Peter, following, went right in and stared.* But the message was in code, and poor Peter, still blind from his dreadful sin on Friday, could only read ABC. He departed wondering, and then John went in, SAW* and believed. Happy John, going thus straight forward to

* Three different verbs in Greek.

faith, without the help of sight. How was it? Surely this: Peter and John had both witnessed the Transfiguration, but only John had later stood by the Cross and heard the *Tetelestai*. Now in the empty tomb the one experience fitted into the other as key fits into lock. The grave-clothes were lying in their folds: and it was obvious that no mortal body, alive or dead, could have got or have been got out of such bandages without undoing them and spilling the spices. Mere re-animation of the body was therefore as untenable an explanation of the facts as its theft. But a *transfigured* Body, such as John had seen on the Mount, could, like the light that it radiated, *pass through* the grave-clothes and leave them undisturbed. Here, then, was the logical sequel to the Second Adam's willing death, here was the conquest of the Strong One with his own best weapon, here was the 'Amen' of the Father to the 'It is finished' of the Son.

Here, too, in the grave-clothes and the empty tomb is the first ground of our faith in the Resurrection. The second is the Appearances of the Risen Lord. These Appearances are sometimes spoken of as *visions*, a word which conveys to the uninstructed an idea that they were purely subjective, like the things one sees in fever, and therefore not real. This is a perversion, because visions in the true sense are glimpses of God, and He is much more real than anything that comes within the reach only of the bodily senses. The Old Testament is full of visions,—how could it be otherwise, since it is the record of revelation?—but it is not always clear whether or no they involved ocular perception. We read that God *spake* to Abraham, that the word of the Lord *came* to a prophet, that Isaiah *saw* Him high and lifted up, and that His angel *was sent* to Mary; and perhaps only in the third of these four examples can we be certain that there was outward vision, such as was granted later to the shepherds on the Bethlehem hills. In *every* case, however, some truth was apprehended upon which the recipient had to act: the vision was at once revelatory and vocational.

The Appearances of the Risen Lord were visions in the completest possible sense: there was outward perception by the senses and there was inward understanding and mission. They are in the same category with the visions given under the Old Covenant and with those of later times, whether the seer be Saul at Damascus gate, John on Patmos, the lady who saw the Lord walking behind His servant Edward Pusey on Didcot platform, or one's ultra-ordinary self, knowing of a surety that certain things are and must be done. But in another way the Appearances were quite unique alike in content and purpose, for That which was shown had but newly come into being, the vision was given only during the Forty Days, and those who saw it had a peculiar function to fulfil in its regard. Imagine a world peopled entirely with intelligent caterpillars, a world to which turning chrysalis had always meant the *end* of life. Imagine a few of its inhabitants suddenly confronted with *one of themselves*, recently pupated, in the form of a butterfly; and that the butterfly says to them, 'As I am, so shall ye be; go, *tell*,'—and you have some idea of the novelty of the apostolic experience.

With that in mind, let us return to Easter Day. The sun is well up now, the joy-bells of Paradise have been ringing since three o'clock on Friday, nature in her spring glory is shouting of the Resurrection, it is time that the voice of man joined the chorus. But in every way the last were first and the first last that day, though all had the same reward in the end; for while the apostles still waited like the empty waterpots at Cana for the sight of Him that filleth all in all, Jesus appeared first to Mary Magdalen, out of whom He had cast seven devils. That was her First Prize for faithfulness on Friday.

His words to her, as she flung herself at His feet in the first rapture of tardy recognition, are commonly taken as a rebuke, an intimation that the old familiar intercourse might not be resumed. But the words are patent of a gentler sense, and one that throws light not on this Appearance only but on all. The first verb, being in the Present Imperative, has a frequentative force: 'Do not keep on touching Me'; and the second, being in the Perfect with a negative, implies that though in the purely historic sense of the Aorist Our Lord had already brought humanity to its goal, the *results* of that Ascension were not yet operative. The Death, Resurrection and Ascension of Jesus were in actual fact but one event, as the rending of the veil at the moment of the first betokens; but for the sake of the finite creatures whom they served they were separated in time by intervals, the first of the inside of three days and the second of forty. The first gave time to those on whom He was to build His Church to know themselves unutterably poor without Him: the second taught them by degrees that their immeasurable richness in possessing Him was independent of sight, so that, when the Forty Days were over, they would be ready for their life-work, and even the Magdalen would not weep.

In the afternoon of Easter Sunday, the Risen Lord went for a walk, thereby sanctifying walks to our use, as later by the lakeside He sanctified picnics. In the guise of a stranger newly come to Jerusalem, He attached Himself to two friends, who were walking to ease the anguish of mind which the morning's rumours had rendered only more acute; and with exquisite and tenderest humour elicited from them the story of His own Passion and the hopes that it had wrecked. Then He spoke. '*Ought* not the Christ to suffer these things and to enter into His glory?' Of course He ought: suffering is the instrument of redemption. You notice that He says '*the Christ.*' Not only is the identity of Messiah and Suffering Servant taken for granted, but the means are seen in relation to the end. In Bernard Shaw's *Saint Joan* there is a scene in which the Maid, twenty-five years dead, appears in a dream to Charles, her sometime Dauphin.   Charles thinks at once of her martyrdom and asks 'Did it hurt much?' 'Did what hurt much?' says Joan.   'Being burnt,' he answers, and Joan says 'Oh, *that!* . . .' and passes on in a moment to enquire about the fruits of her passion in the establishment of his kingdom.   So, as for the joy that was set before Him He had endured on Friday, the Risen Lord sees now of the travail of His soul and is satisfied, remembering no more the anguish.

Now follow the experience of Cleopas and his friend. The Stranger substantiates His question by taking them right through the Scriptures.   The seed of the woman, the curse in which man's fall involved the earth lifted by His own thorny crown, Isaac offered on Moriah, Joseph sold and saving, the Paschal lamb, the prophet like unto Moses, Balaam's Star, the shoot from the old tree-stump of the royal line, the Suffering Servant, the Day of Atonement, the heavenly Messiah of the apocalypses, Bethel, Tabernacle and Temple where God dwells with men, all the tesserae of type and prophecy come together and the figure that they form is Jesus.   The moonlight landscape of the Old Testament has become instinct with life and colour, sunlit, unified, intelligible.   Their intolerable restlessness has given place to peace.   Yet they have not yet asked the Stranger's name, nor do they now: only that He will stay with them and not go away.   And thus it was that in the action that symbolised His mission He was known of them at last.   Intellectual conviction was crowned by one glorious, satisfying moment of open vision.

When the two friends, their supper unfinished, reached Jerusalem with their news, they were met by the tidings that Peter also had seen the Lord.   Probably they would have learnt as much from Peter's face in a minute, had there been time to look; but while they yet spake, there in the midst was Jesus, saying '*Peace*.' 'And,' says S. Luke, 'they were terrified and affrighted and supposed that they had seen a spirit.' Their faith in His Christhood and in the fact that He lived stopped short as yet of His bodily resurrection; they believed themselves to be in the presence only of a ghost.

We can hardly be wrong in taking this story in S. Luke as a complementary version of that dated by S. John at the same time. It is the glory of the Resurrection narratives that they agree completely in regard to the main characteristics of the Appearances, and differ in details exactly as the accounts of independent witnesses always do differ, because no two minds register quite the same impressions. This appearance to the ten,—and apparently some others,—on the evening of Easter Day is really the central one of all, because in it the purpose and consequences of the Resurrection are most clearly manifested. Our Lord is confronted with the nucleus of His seed, the foundations of His church; and His first care is to establish them. Accommodating Himself to their needs, He gives them utmost sensible proof of the reality of His risen Body and of its identity with that in which He suffered. *But He does not explain it.* Then, as now, it is the *fact* of the Resurrection that is important, not its manner: nobody yet knows the laws that govern risen bodies. Yet there are analogies in nature, simple enough. It surely was no accident that Our Lord was born on the Feast of the Sun and rose on its day; and one cannot help thinking that if people in later ages had pondered the properties of sunlight or watched the metamorphoses of insects, they would at any rate not have burnt each other over the manner of the Eucharistic Presence. Still more is the mystery made easy for us, who are told that matter and radiation are but differing forms of energy, who know something of the secrets of the universe and have actual experience of such wonders as wireless and television.

But to return to Easter evening. The Lord elicited from the apostles faith in His Resurrection, but He did not say one word about the past. In His message to them by the women that morning He had already, for the first and only time on record, called them His *brethren*. Yet it was not as brethren that they had behaved when they parted from Him in Gethsemane. It was as much as to say, 'That was not the real you, I know you better than that,' and by His faith in them He generated theirs in Him, and by that faith they were justified, that is, accounted righteous by reason of that which in itself was His gift, part of the 'free bounty' that His tremendous, forgiving, trusting love was pouring into them. Here, then, is the New Covenant in action, the Covenant of *grace*. There is no longer question of any *claim* on God, such as under the Old Covenant was felt to accrue from observance of the Law.* The sufficiency is all on God's side, and men have nothing apart from what He gives. The waterpots are full indeed now, full of life-giving wine; but it is against the law of the universe for anything to be self-contained. The apostles are called to be not pots only but pipes; they are the first instalment of God's irrigation-system for this dried-up world. So Jesus, Who by taking the man-hood into God has made it the inexhaustible reservoir of life for all creation, pronounces to these newly-shriven penitents their commission, 'As the Father hath sent Me, even so send I you. . . . Receive ye Holy Spirit: whose soever sins ye forgive they are forgiven, whose soever sins ye retain they are retained.'

Thus as members and extenders of the New Humanity the apostles took their unique places in line directly after the Head.

There is no connected record of the apostles' experience during the rest of the Great Forty Days. We know only three great facts: that on Low Sunday again the last were

* Cp. p. 49.

K

first and doubting Thomas first confessed the risen Lord as *God;* that Jesus talked on several occasions with them on matters relating to the Kingdom; and that the last Appearance was such as showed plainly no more were to be expected. Like so many things, it was both history and symbol; and the Creed expresses it by saying that 'He ascended into Heaven and sitteth (mark the tense) at the right hand of God.' Historically, the apostles witnessed a visible ascent of the Lord from a mountain-top (how much *that* means!) until a cloud received Him out of their sight. Symbolically the Ascension betokened the mystery already consummated on Good Friday,—the arrival of the perfected Manhood at its home in God. However certain you may be that heaven is a state and not a place, you may still learn a great deal about heaven from contemplating *the* heavens and the place of our little earth in that vast organic unity. Think of God as Himself enwrapping the universe rather than as resident in any part of it, by all means; but do not regard the language of the Creed as childish. To express realities beyond our present experience we have to borrow words from the nearest thing to it, a thing related to the other perhaps as a map of the world is to the world itself. It is the best that can be done, and it always has been done. If you define heaven as where God reigns undisputed and adored, it is easy enough to see in what sense the Word came down from heaven, taught us to pray that His Father's Kingdom might come on earth as it is in heaven, and Himself ascended thither to reign at the Father's right hand. But do not cavil at the metaphors, for you cannot improve upon them.

Putting together the closing verses of S. Matthew and S. Luke and the opening paragraph of the Acts, you find connected with the Ascension two commands, to wait and to go; two promises, of Holy Spirit and of the Lord's own Return; and one statement of present and abiding fact: 'Lo I *am with you* all the days, even unto the end of the age.' Round these five things centres all that we have still to consider in this book.

CHAPTER XVII

THE CHRISTIAN CHURCH

(i) Its Birth and Equipment

IN Ezekiel's vision of the Valley of Dry Bones the miracle of restoration is accomplished in two stages: first, by the Word of the Lord through the prophet they are reintegrated as individuals, and then by the Breath from the four winds evoked by the prophet at God's command, they are made individually dynamic and corporately an effective army.* The hundred and twenty going home after the Ascension are at the first stage. Take a good look at them, for they are important. They are the faithful remnant of the day,— or part of it, for did not five hundred once see the Risen Lord?—they are the nucleus of the New Humanity on earth, and they include not only the eleven apostles and the blessed Mother but a number of other very interesting people. Scripture mentions besides the women only Matthias and Joseph Justus; tradition adds the Bethany family, the widow's son from Nain, the man born blind, and of course Nicodemus and Joseph of Arimathea,— leaving about ninety-five unnamed. All these people had shared in Our Lord's Passion and Resurrection; they had learnt out of their own experience that the way to life is through death, and that it was through Jesus, Who had Himself attained the risen life through the birthpangs of death, that to them also this new birth had come. They depended upon Him as upon God, because He had proved Himself in their experience utterly dependable. All called Him Lord: Thomas, if the Fourth Gospel be taken literally, had in one supreme moment named Him both Lord and God; and of all the Messianic titles provided by their

* Cp. pp. 19-21, about the twofold manifestation of God's creative activity, in objects and in events.

Jewish background 'Son of God' was the one that best expressed Him.   Yet for all that they were still monotheists strictly and only in the Old Testament sense.   Though to worship Jesus as they worshipped God, Whose gift and messenger He was, was the only possible reaction to the facts of experience, they had as yet nor cause nor time nor power to think out the doctrinal implications of their action.   They had no notion yet that the very perfection of the Divine Unity lay in its Plurality of Persons.   Before that basic paradox could even dawn, they must be enlightened and empowered by a new experience of God.

For that reason they, all eager to be up and doing, were told to *wait*.   'Stay in the city,'—the word is sit or be seated, really, just what you would expect of bodies not yet empowered for action,—'until you be clad with power from the height.'   The word translated 'power' is *dunamis*, whence our words dynamic and dynamite, and 'the height' is a Hebraism meaning the highest heaven, a metonym for God.   This was not the first that they had heard of 'the promise of the Father' which was to follow the Lord's going away, first in death and then in visible presence at the Ascension.   Jesus had spoken both of the Holy Breath of God Who was to teach them all things and of the Paraclete or One-called-in-to-help-you, Who is the Holy Breath,—language which to us is plainly personal, but it was not yet so to the hundred and twenty.   To them the Breath or Spirit of God carried its Old Testament meaning, never more clearly evidenced than in Ezekiel's vision, of His life-giving power.

The promise of the Spirit, then, led them to expect from God a new creation.   So they waited, believing, for the blessing that obedience could not fail to bring. 'And when the day of Pentecost was fully come, they were all with one accord in one place.'

Between Passover and Pentecost, the fiftieth day after it, intervened seven weeks of seven days, the square of the perfect number; and in relation to the Passover everything about the Feast of Pentecost spoke of completion. It marked the final ingathering of the corn harvest, of which the first sheaf had been offered at Passover;* and it commemorated the making of the Covenant at Sinai, which was the object and outcome of the Great Deliverance. But considered separately Pentecost bore also the character of inception: for just as harvest is itself a means to an end in the life of man, so was the gathering of the Chosen People into Covenant relationship only a stage in the fulfilment of God's plan,—the institution to his office of the *paidagōgos*, who through thirteen centuries was to lead men to Christ.†

In regard to this paradox of completion and inception the analogy between type and antitype is very close. The descent of Holy Spirit, first on that expectant band and later through Baptism on the three thousand, is the Ascension in the Perfect tense, the fruit-bearing of the corn of wheat that fell into the ground and died on Good Friday. It is this aspect of completion which the fire symbolises, for fire was the sign of God's acceptance of sacrifice. It had been so at Sinai, therefore the parting flames at Pentecost linked the coming of the Spirit at once with the Covenant which it superseded and with the supreme Sacrifice whence it was derived. In terms of Ezekiel's vision, again, Pentecost is the completion of the miracle of restoration, by which the army, hitherto static, becomes through the power of the Breath living and active. But the symbol of the wind carries you over at once from completion to inception, for wind is always moving, life means progress and the *raison-d'être* of an army is to fight and win. So we are faced with a recreative Act of God, similar and successive to that which He wrought on Lady Day: a new creation has been brought out of the old, the New Humanity that centres in Jesus has taken the field

* One of the three feasts referred to on p. 52.   † Cp. p. 48.

as His redemptive instrument. And this new Chosen
People thus conceived by the Holy Ghost of Abraham's
seed bears, as no created thing save the Sacred Humanity
itself has ever borne it, the threefold seal of the Divine
likeness, individual, social and creative. By virtue of the
Spirit-effected union of each human individual with the
Incarnate Word Who is the Head, the many members are
one Body, of the essence of whose nature it is that it should
reproduce its kind. In relation to the old, the New
Humanity is like leaven cast into the lump of dough,
which gradually assimilates all to itself.

But how exactly does it work?

In the simplest way imaginable. For some people, later
developments obscure this simplicity, so it is well to note
that, just as the body of an infant contains in germ the
reproductive organs of the adult, so the new-born Church
of Pentecost has within her,—and operative too,—the
seed of all the means by which she is to grow: she is, in a
sense wholly good, institutional from birth. First,
corresponding to the rite of Initiation under the Old
Covenant, there is Baptism: the individual turning with
his will from sin to Jesus is washed with water in Jesus'
Name; by that act,—the counterpart of the sprinkling with
sacrificial blood,—his sin is forgiven and by power of
Holy Spirit he, justified by his faith alone, like the returning
prodigal, is incorporated into the New Humanity, made
free of the riches of the Messianic Kingdom, and enabled
for the new righteousness which belongs to it. Then the
life of Jesus thus imparted is renewed and quickened in
the initiate through the instrumentality of bread and wine
in the Eucharist, given by the hands of those appointed
so to do,—a specialisation of function within the Body,
which seems to have been rigorously respected from the
first. For the rest, the Christian lives by his prayer: there is
nothing formal or complicated about it, it is just the expression of the fact that he depends on Jesus and His indwelling

Spirit for his inward life, just as for his bodily life he
depends on breathing. And since he is part of a whole,
he will pray often in community,—using, no doubt, those
psalms of the elder Church that, chameleon-like, take on
the colour of his every need,—so that each and all may
be sustained in the faith and love and obedience which
are life. You can find all this in a few verses in Acts;
and you will not find, nor need to find much more anywhere.

Then *why* is it such a big drop from the heights of Pentecost to the plains of Church History? Why, even in
New Testament times, is the actual so unideal, why do
Paul and Barnabas quarrel over Mark, why does Peter,—
of all people,—turn coward over eating with Gentiles, why
are neophytes in Galatia or at Corinth disloyal, petty,
immoral and, worst of all, wholly oblivious apparently
of the New Commandment which is the hall-mark of the
Church?

Let us grasp the nettle at once, for that is the only way
to prevent it stinging. We have seen that the way of the
Kingdom is embodied in Messiah's life-story, that as He
is, so are we in this world. The difference only is this,
that whereas Jesus as Man progressed and effected redemption not only in spite but actually by means of the sins of
others, we have to progress and work out our salvation
by means also of our own. The shortest distance between
two points is a straight line: such was the earthly life of
Jesus. But the further point can also be reached in time
by a zigzag line, provided that the general tendency of
the aberrations *is in the right direction*. Such is the life of
the Church as a whole, and in greater or less degree of
every individual in it. Think of that Way of Holiness
from the *cul-de-sac* to the mountain-top as a narrow path
hedged in, for that is how Our Lord Himself describes it:
it is translated 'straitened' in the Revised Version, and

the actual word is *tethlimmenē*, a Perfect participle implying that the present straitness is the result of obstacles and limitations put there, whether through others' agency or our own, before we came along. Then turn to the Apocalypse, and you find S. John describing the host of the redeemed as those who have come out of the great *thlipsis*, —a noun from the same root as *tethlimmenē*,—and have washed their robes and made them white in the blood of the Lamb,—the which of course implies that they were not white to start with.

It is the old theme of the Suffering Servant and of the Stronger vanquishing the Strong with his own weapons; and the Church as a whole and every microcosm of it, whether it be national church, diocese, parish or the individual soul, is the stage on which that drama is continually re-enacted: it is these recurring rhythms which make up the symphony of Restoration. That is why for the individual now, as during the Incarnate Life on earth, everything depends on ability to recognise and respond to the real thing in the most unlikely forms and places. The Divine demand is still for that *faith* which is inseparable from love and cannot issue otherwise than in obedience. It is difficult, of course. It is tiring to be a battlefield and to live on a battlefield, where the old Adam and the New strive for the mastery like Rebekah's twins. But *ought* not the Christian to suffer these things and, transmuting them by thankful acceptance, to enter into his glory?

Then there is another thing. The Church History of which we have cognisance is only external and partial. Take illustrations. When a great building is being erected behind a hoarding, passers-by get all the noise and dirt, but see nothing of the work. Those engaged on it get still more noise and dirt and do not see very much, only each his little bit. But one day the noise and dirt cease, the workmen lay down their tools, the hoarding is taken down and the building is seen, perfect. Again, imagine some great open space like Salisbury Plain, and on it one vast building, many storeys high, each more brilliantly lit, it may be, than the last, and full of people. In the porch, which is but dimly lit, there are a few more people. There is a constant stream passing into the porch from the darkness of the surrounding night, and out of the porch into the house. But the only place where you can watch their doings is the porch itself. Which same truth that the fighting Church is but part of a greater whole was expressed long ago by the author of Hebrews in the metaphor of the amphitheatre, with this difference from the earthly counterpart, that the cloud of witnesses of which he speaks, had themselves experienced the blood and dust of the arena.

Quite early in this book, we stood in imagination behind faithful Abraham as he set out for Canaan, and envisaged the journey that lay before his seed. Now as we stand on the quay and watch the fishing-smack of Pentecost, with Abraham's seed on board, sail off, nets spread, on her voyage through the ages, the task is harder, for a sea-course does not show so plainly as a road on land, and the haven is not yet reached. Still it is worth the effort. First, you watch her through four centuries of choppy seas, consolidating within and extending without to and beyond the confines of the Roman Empire,—noticing, by the way, that when she first puts out there are no sea-birds, but the further she goes the greater the wheeling flock that follows the same course in the higher element. Next she enters the confused and rocky passage of the Dark Ages, at strife within herself and menaced from without on one side by the surges of heathenism and on the other by the pirate ship of Islam. In the eleventh century you see to your horror that the ship, which has been growing steadily in size since she set out, has now two decks, between which there is no commerce.

Four turbulent centuries follow and then a fearful

period of storm and upheaval, from which the ship emerges as a three-decker with a flotilla of small but unsociable craft alongside: a little more and you find your view is constricted, because you yourself are on the ship, looking out of a bow porthole on the middle deck at the uncharted ocean ahead.

That is as far as we can see. Nobody can possibly tell how much longer the Church must plough her course through the waves of this world before she gets to port. The Last Days have already lasted nineteen hundred years, and she has had a rough voyage. The waves of the sea are mighty and rage horribly,—not least in our own time,—but yet the Lord, the Truth Dependable that dwelleth on high, is mightier.

CHAPTER XVIII

THE CHRISTIAN CHURCH

(ii) Its Growth to Maturity under the Roman Empire

THESE Last Days, whose course to the present has just been figuratively reviewed, extend as yet over scarcely so long a period as that between Abraham and the Incarnation, which we have already considered. But they are for two reasons much more difficult to sum up; not only is the scene of action vastly wider, but the drama which we watch is still in progress, and it is hard to get the final scene in true perspective, because we ourselves are part of it. These next five chapters are, therefore, the most impossible part of an impossible book. It would be much easier not to write or read them; but then the book would not be THE WOOD. So the attempt must be made, not just to chase Church History over the map like lumps of mercury that will not coalesce; but by tracing the main lines of development that link Pentecost to the present day, to satisfy ourselves that the fire which Our Lord cast on the earth in A.D. 29 burns still, victorious and unquenchable, and that beneath appearances the process of Restoration goes forward 'according to plan.'

It is much easier to understand Church History if you remember that it is in the nature of living things to *grow*, and that growth is stimulated and conditioned by environment. The Church at birth, few in numbers and entirely Jewish in composition, possessed historical experience of Jesus, a handful of officials appointed by Him and certain clear but general instructions for carrying on; and just because it was a living body, abidingly indwelt by the Holy Spirit and destined to be coextensive with the whole human race, all those germinal resources were bound to grow. The Apostles' witness to the facts of the Incarnate Life on earth was necessary to establish the faith of Jesus on its historical basis; but that experience was even for them only the prelude to the deeper spiritual experience of Him through the Spirit, to which others were and are admitted directly through Baptism. Under the guidance of the Spirit and in response to the call of circumstances the implications of the initial experience had to be progressively drawn out: the Ministry must develop as the Society grew, the faith must be formulated for transmission to all nations, and the conditions of the administration of the Sacraments 'ordained by Christ Himself' must be determined in relation to the needs of men.

This process of growth and adaptation is still going on, because the needs of men vary with place and race, and the store whence God brings out His treasures old and new is inexhaustible. But the broad outlines of the Church's faith and practice were determined within five centuries of her birth, during the time when by divine arrangement she was mainly situated within the Roman Empire; and that is the period to be reviewed in this chapter.

Of it, the New Testament covers only about thirty-five years, but how much development it shows! Before the Apostles leave Jerusalem, they ordain the seven deacons, set them in rank after themselves as sharers of the authority which the Twelve received from Jesus. The immediate occasion of the deacons' appointment was the need of extra hands for distributing the common fund, which just shows how right it is that spiritual functions and those which we are pleased to call material should be exercised conjointly. Then Herod, prompted by hostile Jews, attempts to disperse the new Society, with the result that the deacon Philip extends it greatly by a mission in Samaria.

There also it appears that the Sacrament of Initiation may be received in two parts, and that the Apostles have reserved to themselves the right to administer the second, the laying on of hands which conveys the Holy Spirit. The Church thus developing within her native land comes increasingly into collision with the Jews, to whom the notion of a crucified Messiah is still abhorrent; and thus, though there is no deliberate schism, the distinctness of the child from the parent body becomes gradually more apparent. Christians may and do continue to attend the Temple services and to observe the Sabbath and the Law; but their central act of worship is the Eucharist and their chief holy day in the week is not the seventh but the first, hallowed for ever by Messiah's Resurrection.

And then within five years of Pentecost comes the conversion of Saul of Tarsus, the vessel chosen by Jesus to bear His Name to the Gentiles.

When Jesus was crucified, Pilate caused the title on His cross to be written in three languages, Hebrew, Greek and Latin, so that all the world might know that this man died for calling Himself a king within the bounds of Empire. In Saul of Tarsus the three elements represented by those languages met and mingled, for he was Hebrew by race and religion, Greek by speech and environment, and Latin by citizenship. As a Hebrew he was the acme of the Law's achievement, for the keeping of it brought him, not to peace but to the sense of need of it, to knowledge of the truth expressed in the closing words of the great Law psalm, that man's best efforts are powerless to effect his salvation, it is God who must seek His strayed servant. As a Hellene, he spoke and thought Greek; and that in the first century A.D. meant knowing something about the Mystery religions, those strange cults of Isis, Cybele, Mithras and the rest, so much in vogue in the groping heathen world, which claimed through the secret rites of a *Kurios* or Deliverer to give *salvation*,—inward

peace and deliverance from the fear of death.   And lastly,
Saul of Tarsus was a Roman citizen and proud to be so.
He gloried in the splendid organisation of the Empire
which bound men of all nations into a social entity,
diverse yet one, to whose growing life every race and
every individual could contribute.   With this threefold
background Saul met Jesus outside Damascus and found
in Him the God Holy and Only and the Servant-Christ
of Judaism, the personal Saviour of his own soul and the
Head of that Society of the Saved which, like the Empire,
was to include all men in one whole, individual, social
and creative.

As he had previously tried to dope the pangs of non-
attainment by persecuting the Christians, his conversion
was for him what Good Friday and Easter had been for
the eleven; it was the experience of fall and rising again,
that is, of death and resurrection, which Simeon had foretold for many in Israel as the consequence of contact with
Jesus—the authentic Way of the Kingdom which is the
Way of the King.   And so Saul, broken and re-made,
became of all men most generous and efficient in filling
up that which is lacking of the sufferings of Christ; and
out of that efficiency in suffering sprang all the effectiveness
of his apostolate.   You can scarcely overestimate his work
for the Church.   He evangelised Jews, proselytes and
heathen in many cities of the Empire; he fought for and
won the direct admission of Gentile converts to the New
Covenant; he worked out the implications of the Christian
law of love and purity in a pagan world; he evolved a
unified presentment of the faith of Jesus, pouring Hebrew
revelation into the prepared mould of the Greek language
and reinforcing it with all that was best in pagan thought;
he organised local churches under elders and overseers,—
presbuteroi and episcopoi,—each one of which was a microcosm of the great whole not yet fully realised, the one,
holy, catholic and apostolic Ecclesia of Christ, His Body

upon earth, coextensive with humanity. What a record, achieved by faith in Jesus out of the weakness that is stronger than strength! At the end of his life, S. Paul wrote to Timothy, 'I have fought the good fight,'—the *beautiful* fight, you might translate it,—'I have finished the course, I have kept the faith.' All those verbs are in the Perfect tense, the second, *teteleka*, being the same, in the Active voice and first person, as the Sixth Word from the Cross, the golden *Tetelestai*. Here is exemplified the progressive fruitfulness of the Tree of Calvary, the process by which the redemption, there effected in potential completeness, advances in the Mystical Body to its fulfilled perfection.

S. Paul, together with S. Peter, passes from the scene about A.D. 64. It is an important date, because it is the first persecution of the Church by the State; and that which Nero did then in order to find a scapegoat for his crimes, later emperors for the next two and a half centuries did at intervals from set policy, regarding the Church as a secret society, whose existence was inimical to the common good.* According to tradition, S. Peter won the last round of his life-long battle with cowardice the night before his crucifixion: for S. Paul, who had died so many deaths already, this last death under the headsman's axe seems to have held no terrors; one only wonders whether for once he did not regret his Roman citizenship, since it debarred him from dying on a cross.

The passing of these two great Apostles through the gate of death had great influence on the development of the Church on earth. As few of the original witnesses now remained and the Return of the Lord still delayed, the need was felt for written records to stabilise and conserve the oral tradition of His Life and teaching: hence a multitude

* This was due partly to the Christians' refusal to take part in the prescribed acts of Emperor worship, the only State religion which was of universal obligation on all except the Jews.

of gospels, from which through circumstances and the Holy Spirit our four emerged eventually as canonical.* In the local churches, also, that had no longer an Apostle as visible head, other leaders had to be appointed; and the title *episcopos* or bishop, hitherto interchangeable with *presbuteros*, came to be reserved for the *chief* presbyter only. Records are scanty over the sub-apostolic period, and the exact stages by which the change was effected are not clear. But by the time Ignatius of Antioch, who had been a disciple of John of Ephesus, wrote his seven letters to the Churches of Asia on his way to martyrdom somewhere between A.D. 110 and 117, the threefold ministry of bishop, priest and deacon was established in the Church exactly as we have it now.

The dawn of the second century, which saw the full development of the Apostolic ministry, saw also the full growth of the Baptismal Creeds. Since to be a Christian means primarily to believe in a Person, it was natural that candidates for Baptism should make a profession of faith. You see it happening spontaneously in the story of the Ethiopian eunuch: S. Philip, who may well have talked with Cleopas and his friend, has just explained to him the great chapter about the Suffering Servant; and the man *sees*, as those two saw when the Lord Himself explained it to them on the walk to Emmaus. He wants to be baptised at once, that minute, and S. Philip says, 'If you believe with all your heart, you may.' With shining eyes the black disciple answers, *'I believe that Jesus Christ is the Son of God.'* That includes everything: and it seems that it or the equivalent *'I believe that Jesus is Lord'* was the usual formula in the earliest days. But by the time S. Matthew's gospel was written, somewhere in the seventies of the first century, experience had led the Church

* The Emperor Diocletian helped to fix the canon by making it penal to possess a copy of the Scriptures. Christians then wanted to know what *were* Scriptures, and what one could hand over without becoming a 'traditor.'

to recognise both Son and Spirit as equally God with Him whom the Son called Father; and Baptism was administered not in the Name of Jesus only but in the Threefold Name of Father, Son and Spirit. The catechumen followed suit: he now said 'I believe in God: the Father, the Son Jesus Christ our Lord, and the Holy Spirit' or words to that effect. Round that Trinitarian nucleus there grew short summaries of the faith, scriptural in language, alike in substance, beautifully various in detail. By about A.D. 100 every local Church had one of these home-grown treasures to pass on to subsequent generations of Christians. Our 'Apostles'' Creed is a later form of the one that grew in Rome. It is concise to the point of dryness and deadeningly familiar, especially when monotoned on *G*. But turn your imagination to its eighteen centuries of history on the living lips of men, and it will blossom like the rose.

The internal development of the Church in the second and third centuries was greatly influenced by the Persecutions, one of the chief problems raised being the matter of Discipline. In the earliest days, and so long as only adults were baptised, Baptism meant such complete conversion that the possibility of a man's falling into serious sin *after* it was scarcely envisaged. As time went on, however, such things did occur; and in times of persecution, particularly, men would yield,—offer incense to the gods or hand over scriptures, and then, repenting, seek readmission to the Church. What was to happen? What would Our Lord say about it? The answer was found, after much seeking, in a further subdivision of the Sacrament of Initiation. This, as we saw, consisted of three parts,—forgiveness of sins, incorporation into the Mystical Body, and gift of Holy Spirit, the last being already conveyed separately by the laying on of hands. The essence of Initiation lay in the second part; and a man could not *begin* to be a member of Christ twice over. Re-baptism was therefore out of the question; but since the Divine love knows no limits, there was still the blessed possibility of *re-forgiveness*. Thus the Sacrament of Penance for the remission of post-baptismal sin came into separate existence. In it, whether the confession of sin be made publicly as under primitive conditions, or privately as in later usage, the stress is on the twofold character of the Christian's sin. It is not against God only, but also against the Body of which he is a member. Confession must therefore be made to the Body as well as to God; and of that Body, which includes the whole company of heaven, the congregation in the one case, and in the other the priest who also holds Our Lord's authority to forgive, acts as representative. This new Sacrament met the needs not only of the lapsed but also of the growing number of those who, having been baptised in infancy, had previously had no opportunity for the sacramental remission of actual sin.

     .   .   .   .   .

Mephistopheles in Goethe's *Faust* speaks of himself as the spirit who is always willing evil and effecting good,— always defeating his own object, that is, because the Stronger than he makes use of his weapons. Of no Satanic effort is this more true than of the Decian persecution in the third century. It was particularly fierce in Egypt, and the hinterland of Egypt is the desert, which possesses an equable climate and any amount of caves. Into the desert, to escape persecution, fled the Christians; in the desert they met ascetics who had already retired thither from choice; and the life of poverty and prayer in their company proved so satisfying that, when the persecution ended, many had no wish to return. Thus, less than a century before the lowering of standards consequent upon the establishment of Christianity as the Emperor's religion, was born Monasticism, whose function hereafter was to keep standards up. The Egyptian ventures are associated with the names of Pachomius and Anthony,—Anthony, salt of the earth, who emerged from twenty years' single combat with the devil the sanest and most practical of men, who organised communities that still persist, and whose friendship with the scholar Athanasius,—he himself was illiterate,—is the loveliest and most fruitful in Christian history. But this is anticipating. Between the beginnings of Egyptian monasticism and the friendship of Anthony and Athanasius lies the last great Persecution, which, begun by Diocletian in 304, lasted until the Edict of Constantine in 313.

Diocletian was the Emperor who abandoned the cares of state in order to grow cabbages; and it was the superior attraction of the cabbages which left the later course of the persecution in far less tolerant hands. Diocletian influenced the Church not only by trying to destroy her, but also by dividing into two parts the Empire in which she was situated. Feeling that it was too unwieldy to be ruled effectively from one centre, he conceived the plan of having two capitals, Rome in the West and Nicomedia in the East, each with its own Emperor or Augustus, subserved by a Caesar who would eventually succeed him. Racially and temperamentally the Empire was already divided, for, speaking generally, the West was Latin and practical and the East speculative and Greek, each excellent of itself but needing the other to complete it. Diocletian's plan was a fine one and in an unfallen world it would have worked beautifully. Actually, the strifes and jealousies of the Emperors and their underlings only made confusion worse confounded; and the unhappy relations between East and West in the State were increasingly reflected in the Church. The House of Empire, divided against itself, was bound to fall: for the Church also the tragedy of schism was impending. But while she still held together and before the sheltering arms of Empire were withdrawn, a further phase of her development had to be accomplished,—the formulation of the central doctrine of the Person of Christ.

In the New Testament, S. John had concentrated on the mystery of the Incarnation and S. Paul on that of the Atonement. During the period of the Persecutions, Christian thought had chiefly followed the lead of the former; and various theses and antitheses had been put forward to expand the teaching inherent in the statement that '*the Word was made flesh*.' As we have already seen, living doctrine must grow, and Theology, like any other science, can progress only by a zigzag course. The views which conflicted with the general judgment of the Church were condemned as heresies, that is to say, doctrines which stressed one aspect of the truth to the exclusion of another. You might define a heretic as a person who is incapable of believing a paradox, because he has the old wineskin mentality which cannot stretch to take in both sides.

The most dangerous heretic who ever lived was Arius, a presbyter of Alexandria whose teaching first attracted notice in 319, six years after the cessation of persecution. The trouble with Arius was that his mind worked backwards. Instead of regarding man as made in the image of God, he thought of God as reflecting the image of man, and argued therefore that because a human father exists before his son, it was true to say of God the Son that '*once He was not*.' His Patriarch, who realised the implications of this teaching, took him to task; whereupon Arius, who was an eloquent, attractive person with a passion for being in the middle of the picture, left Egypt and played the injured innocent elsewhere with such effect that Christendom was soon divided into two camps. In 325, the Emperor Constantine, disgusted at the strife among his Christians, bade the Bishops meet and settle their differences in council at Nicaea in Bithynia.

A Council was the right way to meet the difficulty, for synodical government is the natural outcome of the fact that the Church, indwelt by the Spirit, is at once individual and social. You can read about the first Church Council that ever was in Acts xv; and the Council of Nicaea differed from earlier councils in two respects only; it was the first to be convened by a secular authority,—the only power then strong enough to do it,—and it was the first to be regarded subsequently as oecumenical, that is, as universally authoritative in the Church.

Picture the map in 325, when all roads led to Nicaea. From Spain comes the aged Hosius of Cordova, confessor in the persecution, who is to preside. From the East beyond the frontier comes James of Nisibis; from Palestine the historian Eusebius of Caesarea; from Rome two deacons to represent the Pope;* from Cyprus, a strange figure in his sheepskin among that toga-clad throng, the shepherd bishop Spyridon, whose mummy can still be seen; from Egypt, besides the Patriarch Alexander in whose suite is the little deacon Athanasius, two Coptic bishops, one lame because he was hamstrung in the persecution, the other blind of an eye, for he gave it for his faith. And so on. These men, traditionally three hundred and eighteen in number, came together as successors of the Apostles to witness to the traditional faith preserved in every Church. We have fairly full accounts of the proceedings of the Council. Those who saw that the teaching of Arius was really a denial of Our Lord's Divinity still fought like lions to find expression for the true faith in scriptural language. Phrase after phrase was tried, only to be rejected as the Arians twisted it to their own meaning. Finally, in order to safeguard the *sense* of scripture, a word was borrowed from the philosophical language of the day, and a creed, based on two Palestinian baptismal creeds, was drawn up, in which Our Lord was said to be

* The bishops of Rome and Carthage each bore the title Pope or Father.

homo-ousion tō Patri,* of one substance with the Father. This no Arian would accept; and the Creed was signed by all the bishops but six. But the apparent triumph of Catholicism was wrecked by imperial tactlessness: Constantine banished Arius and the six bishops as if they were political offenders, and a fierce reaction arose in their favour, largely among those who did not really understand the point at issue. For forty years Athanasius, who succeeded Alexander in the Patriarchate soon after the Council, stood for the Nicene faith against the world, a long and fruitful passion.

Arianism was the first of a series of errors, each of which evoked Councils and scholar-saints. An application of the same heresy to the Third Person of the Trinity led to the addition at Constantinople† in 381 of all that now follows His title in the Nicene Creed. A little later, Augustine of Hippo did battle with the Manichaean dualism he had once embraced, and out of his own profound experience magnified the Catholic doctrine of grace against the minimising teaching of Pelagius. Somewhat later still, the oecumenical Councils of Ephesus and Chalcedon dealt with the antithesis of Arianism usually associated with the name of Nestorius, applying the title *Theotokos* or Mother of God to Mary to stress the fact that the Eternal Son was also true Man from the first moment of His conception. The Council of Chalcedon in 451 ended the period of theological definition by effecting a synthesis in one formula of both sides of the truth, and the Definition of Chalcedon ranks with the Creed of Nicaea among those standards of Christian faith, with which all subsequent restatements must agree in essence as they themselves agree with Scripture, tradition and experience.

* *homo-* = one and the same, as in *homo*geneous. *Ousia* = essence or *substance* in the literal sense of underlying reality.

† Constantine had moved the Eastern capital to Byzantium and renamed it after himself.

This common work of East and West, more vital than we realise, was accomplished just in time. Already in 410 Italy had been overrun and Rome sacked by the Visigoths under Alaric; in 430, the year before the Council of Ephesus, Augustine died at Hippo while Vandals hammered at its gates; in 451, the year of Chalcedon, the Huns under Attila burst across central Europe. The Roman Empire, nurse, persecutor, protector of the Church, was no more.

CHAPTER XIX

THE CHRISTIAN CHURCH

(iii) East and West from the Fall of Rome to the Great Schism

THE jungle of the Kings of Israel and Judah, viewed in Chapter VIII, was a park compared with the period we now have to traverse. It is as though, with a crash that echoes still, a gigantic tree has fallen, and over the rotten paling that surrounded it, over the effete carcase of the tree itself, there swarms in a forest of saplings, exuberant but barren, for their time of fruit is not yet. The Romans had designated the uncouth, uncleanly hordes who had long menaced their northern frontiers as *barbari* or Jabberers, because these uncultured peoples spoke no language intelligible to the educated ear. The generation that witnessed the Barbarians' triumph, that saw the Western Empire collapse before them like a house of cards, had an experience similar to that of living through an earthquake. Everything stable was moved, everything familiar destroyed. You had either to lose your head and be lost too, or keep it and see what you could possibly rescue out of the ruins.

When this happened, the Church, though she had barely a century of constructive peace behind her since the persecutions, had a proved system of provincial organisation, modelled on that of the Empire and centred in the West at Rome. As successor of S. Peter and S. Paul and bishop of the imperial city, the Pope of Rome had always held a sort of primacy among his brethren, and he had come also to have an appellate jurisdiction over them, that is to say, when difficulties arose that could not be settled at home, the Pope was the natural person to consult. When the Western Empire fell, the Papacy was the only power that remained. It kept its head, set a splendid example of courage and calmness amid the prevailing chaos, earned the uncalculating gratitude of countless people, and so quietly stepped into the shoes of the dead Empire. Practice being established, theory followed. It was said that Our Lord's words to S. Peter, 'On this rock I will build My Church,' meant that the successor of S. Peter was intended by Him to hold an authoritative jurisdiction over the whole Church, claiming as His vice-regent its universal obedience.

Meanwhile, the Patriarch of the sister-capital of Constantinople was in a very different position. In the East the shadow of an Empire still persisted; and later Emperors went further than Constantine in regarding the Church as a department of the state, and themselves as competent theological authorities. The Easterns had always believed that the Church was meant to be autocephalous, each part under its own head and matters of general importance being settled by the bishops in council. With this view papal primacy was compatible; with papal supremacy it was not. Small wonder that the Eastern Patriarch, tied to the imperial apron-strings, looked with jealous disapproval at his free and pushful brother in the West.

Wheat and tares, wheat and tares, and the Lord says that both are to grow together till the harvest. With the shadow of the coming schism growing ever darker, each side of Christendom battled manfully with its several problems. The West had to conserve Christian order and morality and the shreds of civilisation in a licentious and uncultured world: above all it had to evangelise the Barbarians. Some of these were more or less Christian already: the Goths, for instance, had been converted to a mild form of Arianism in the fourth century by the valiant old bishop Wulfila, who reduced their lovely, virile language to writing and translated into it all the Bible except the warlike Books of Kings; the Lombards, too, were Arians, though of a more aggresive type. But many tribes, including all the Teutons from the north, were rank heathen. See then the missionary problem as it faced Pope Gregory at the end of the sixth century. The Roman road system was in decay, the prevailing lawlessness made travel dangerous; there was no longer any common language save Latin, which the barbarians did not know; books were extremely scarce and hardly anybody could read. Yet the Lord Who bade 'Go, teach' Himself provided the instruments. A century and a half before, Athanasius on his third exile had stayed at Rome in company with two Egyptian monks, and had there talked of his friend Anthony of the Desert. The West, thus fired by the East, began to develop its own forms of the Religious Life. At the close of the fifth century, an Italian boy named Benedict was sent to Rome to be educated. Terrified by the evil he saw there, he fled to a cave, whence, having stablished his own soul, he emerged in manhood to gather into one Rule the stored wisdom of all previous ascetics and to found the greatest Religious Order of all time. To it Gregory himself belonged: from it went out missionaries beyond number, among them Gregory's friend and emissary Augustine, who landed in Kent with his companions in 597.

As this is the mission to which we English owe our Christianity, it is well to look at it closely, and to see how authentic and continuous it is, this planting of Jerusalem in our beloved England. To tackle the 'barbarous, fierce and unbelieving nation,' which since the withdrawal of the legions had occupied our island, was a costly venture of faith and obedience. There was indeed a moment on the journey when the missionaries felt they could not face it, and sent Augustine back to Gregory to say so. Augustine came back with the full authority of Abbot, so the little band which plucked up its courage and went on was a Religious community, a microcosm of the Church in its threefold character, individual, social and creative. Bede's account of their activities on arrival reads like a page from Acts,—prayer, common life, Eucharist, evangelism. A few months later, Augustine wrote back to Gregory for instruction on certain matters which had cropped up. One question related to certain 'clerks' attached to his own party who were not monks and were only in minor orders. These young men are obscure but interesting. Every monastery had a school within its walls, the boys of which provided the treble portion of the monastic choir; and these clerks may quite possibly have been such trebles grown to tenors. We should not take young choirmen on a pioneer mission ourselves, of course, but then we have not got the Dark Ages' sense of the central importance of worship. Anyhow, Gregory was emphatic that these boys must be kept under rules and *attend to the singing of psalms*,' that is, to the Divine Office, the Benedictine Work of God. Here is a side-issue worth exploring, for it throws light on the whole period. The psalms of course were Hebrew, inherited from the elder Church and sung now in the venerable Latin. But the *music*, despite its Greek affinities, was in spirit uniquely and supremely Christian, a language born of the mysteries and growing with their apprehension. Already in the fourth century there was in the Church a traditional body of this 'sung prayer'; this Gregory himself in the sixth had edited and developed; this his sons brought to England,—they seem to have been always singing, according to Bede;—and his sons' sons in every monastery of Europe passed on to subsequent generations—aurally, for the most part,—as a very precious heritage, growing, indeed, yet as sacred and inviolable in its essence as the very Canon of Scripture. If you can understand what Western monks from the sixth to the eleventh centuries felt about their Plainchant, you have seen what was the secret glory of the Dark Ages in a hundred spheres. For without that spirit of conservation, that amazing faithfulness in preserving intact the common treasure, there could have been no subsequent revival of enlightenment and no modern civilisation.

Augustine, journeying to England through what had been Roman Gaul, travelled through a country that had been nominally Christian for a hundred years. The follow-my-leader spirit was strong among the Teutons; and when in 496 Clovis, king of the Franks was baptised by S. Remigius, his tribesmen were baptised with him as a matter of course. Nor was it very far otherwise with Ethelbert, whose queen was Clovis' granddaughter, and the people of Kent. In England the Latin Christianity introduced by Augustine met and ultimately absorbed to its own enrichment the remains of the Romano-British Church which had persisted among the Celts, probably since the first century. But even under the best conditions, the evangelisation of the barbarian races was of necessity very sketchily effected. A little new Christianity was scattered over the ancient field of heathenism; with the few it went deep, but the many, like the bulk of the Israelites in Elijah's time, saw no vital difference between the new religion and the old. The result was a childish sort of religious syncretism which makes the history of the Dark Ages unfit reading for any who have forgotten what it feels like to be a child. Nobody at that time was really grown-up, and it is as absurd to judge its peoples' apprehension of the faith by that of the Fathers of the fourth century as it would be to examine a First Form child by the standard of the Sixth. You see the mentality of the age exemplified in its greatest figure,—Charlemagne. He was king of the Franks at the end of the eighth century and a most fervent Christian. He is credited with the authorship of the *Veni Creator Spiritus*, and he also made laws which imposed the death penalty equally for killing a bishop and for eating meat in Lent. He also formed a noble plan for restoring to Western Europe the vanished order of Rome; he and the Pope as respectively the temporal and the spiritual head were to rule it conjointly; and Charlemagne believed quite seriously that this was what Our Lord had meant when He said of the two swords offered to Him in Gethsemane, 'It is enough.' Though he meant gloriously well and effected much, his plan, actualised on Christmas Day, 800, failed in the long run as Diocletian's plan had failed, through the strifes of the joint rulers. Moreover, the establishment of the new régime under the title of the Holy Roman Empire widened the breach between the two sides of Christendom, for it completely ignored the ancient Roman Empire still existing in the East, and the great Church within its borders.

The Eastern Church had trouble enough already. Just about the time that Augustine was evangelising Kent, an Arabian camel-driver of the name of Mohammed or Mahomet had believed himself called to be the prophet of monotheism against idolatry. It is at least possible that this was really so, and that through self-interest he subsequently took a wrong turning. The devil has no stronger instrument than a perverted vocation. Mohammed built his creed largely on Jewish foundations: he regarded Abraham as the father of the faithful, and Our Lord as a prophet, though much less great than himself. There were of course no idols, but there was also no Trinity, no Incarnation, no Redemption and no moral standard of inconvenient height. The followers of Mohammed formed a militant missionary society, a parody and rival of the Church. The birth of this new faith at the doors of Eastern Christendom did more than hinder its expansion, it gave rise also to acute internal dissension. Since the Christianisation of the Empire, the East had used *ikons*, sacred pictures in bas-relief, just as freely as the West had used ordinary pictures and statues. When the Moslem attack on idolatry began, the Eastern Emperor and some brow-beaten Church officials decided that the ikons were in themselves of the nature of idols and must be abolished. In this they were backed by the army, but the Church as a whole, led by the monks, stood to it that the ikons were a means to devotion, not its end, that they were the books of the unlearned and, further, that the fact of God having appeared in visible form in the Incarnation rendered obsolete the letter of the second commandment. In the end the Church won, but it was a bitter and exhausting struggle.

Nor was that the end of matters with Islam: the Church's very existence also was threatened. The Arab tribes which formed the original following of the Prophet spread rapidly round the Mediterranean. In Asia Minor and Palestine they occupied the ground of early Christianity, and shook their fists across the Bosphorus at Constantinople itself. The once illustrious Church of North Africa, weakened already by barbarian invasions, also went down before them; and from Africa the Moors, as they came to be called, passed over into Spain, and once even crossed the Pyrenees into France, though Charlemagne's grandfather saw to it that they never came again. But though the enemies of the East were now the enemies also of the West, East and West did not co-operate in fighting them. The linguistic and temperamental difference on which Diocletian had based the division of his realm was reflected in Orthodox and Papal Christendom and enhanced by the fall of imperial Rome, by the growing claims of the Papacy, by the establishment of the Holy Roman Empire, and by a thousand circumstances, molehills in themselves, which lack of love on either side magnified into mountains. For over two hundred years after the time of Charlemagne the two great Churches, that are one Church, united on all the cardinal points of faith and practice, continued mutually unable to see straight where the other was concerned. In 1054, the long tension crystallised into the Great Schism, which is still unhealed. Each at his central altar, Pope and Patriarch declared the other excommunicate, the latter adding 'May God look on it and judge.'

It is a poor, crippled Ship that ploughs the waves now, with the crews of her two decks thus estranged. She moves slowly, by a zigzag course, with much damage, many encounters with the rocks and much interruption of her business. Yet she is still one Ship, making for port. The Mystical Body of Jesus, like that in which He died, though wounded, is not broken.

CHAPTER XX

THE CHRISTIAN CHURCH

(iv) Western Christendom in the Middle Ages

FROM the eleventh century to the fifteenth the barbarian races in Western Europe were in their adolescence; and their tutor was the Roman Church. The absence of any strong central power in things temporal makes the period almost as difficult to follow as it must have been to live in; all that can be done is to trace through the half-tamed jungle those narrow tracks of progress which expand later into the broad though bloody highways of the sixteenth and following centuries.

This progress, whatever its limitations, was effected in the authentic Christian way by means of obstacles. The many evils of the Middle Ages resulted chiefly from three causes—the pugnacity and limited outlook of the schoolboy nations, whose ancestors had become Christian under such unideal conditions; the maladjustment of Church and State, and the presence at the heart of the Christian world of hostile Islam.

Take the Crusades first. When in the eleventh century the comparatively tolerant Arab was replaced in Palestine by the fanatic Turk, the Christian visited the Holy Places only at the risk of his life. At the same time there was a religious revival afoot in Western Europe, which had originated in the previous century in the Benedictine Monastery of Cluny, in Burgundy; so when Pope Urban II in 1095 sounded the call to arms on behalf of the Holy Places, he met with a tremendous response. Men in the Middle Ages were fundamentally religious, they never made the mistake of thinking that sin did not matter or that this life was all. But they did look to save their souls largely by *works*, and to take the Cross appeared an excellent way of doing it, while to encourage others to take it was for the harassed potentate a still more excellent way of getting rid of inconvenient nobles. The wars thus begun continued at intervals for two and a half centuries, but only for a very short time were the Holy Places in Christian hands. Other results, however, ensued, as mixed as the motives of the Crusaders. The prestige of the Papacy was heightened, for to it the Crusades owed their being; Eastern Christendom was further estranged by the establishment in its territory of Latin Patriarchates at Jerusalem and Antioch; Eastern civilisation was brought home to the uncultured West, mental horizons began to stretch. *And who knows how many souls were saved, however ignorant and foolish, because they did what they believed to be God's will, unsparing of the cost to themselves? The real spiritual history of the Crusades will not be written in this world.*

Another line of progress belongs to the monastic world. The Religious Orders, whose function is to conserve and cherish the things men live by, are themselves composed of sinful men. The spiritual quality of an Order fluctuates; at one time the life burns low; then, by the Indwelling Spirit Whose it is, revives to meet fresh needs. Movements of reform or of new foundation followed each other like waves across these troubled centuries, each with its untold tale of sainthood and salvation. Such were the Cluniac movement already referred to; the Cistercian, also Benedictine, adorned by S. Bernard; the Augustinian reform begun at the 'pré montré' to S. Norbert;* and the two great movements set going in the thirteenth century by S. Dominic and S. Francis, the apostles respectively of truth and of brotherhood in an ignorant and unloving age.

The monks were not the only people alive to the evils

* Hence the name Premonstratensian.

of the day. The Papacy, for all its preoccupation with
secular affairs and its perennial quarrel with the Emperors,
convened nine Councils within four Centuries for the
purpose of promulgating reform. The Conciliar movement as a whole is accounted a failure, but it was an effort
on the right method and in the right direction by no means
barren of results. One of the Councils, that of Lyons in
1274, discussed the question of reunion with the East,
showing that the evil of schism was at least not acquiesced
in; and that of Constance early in the fifteenth century
concluded the schism within the Papacy itself, which for
seventy-two years had scandalised Christendom and kept
a Pope in exile at Avignon. And so on.

And all the time beneath and around these movements,
new life was stirring. Men whose ancestors had wrecked
Rome were looking back to her vanished order and desiring
to re-establish it. You see it in several spheres. In the
twelfth century, the logic of the Greek philosopher
Aristotle, introduced into Europe in Arabic translation
by the Moors, was just becoming known in Latin. One
of the people who read it was a Breton named Abelard,
and it went to his head like new wine. He began to give
fascinating lectures, showing how the principles of logic
might be applied to the mysteries of the Faith. It was a
risky line of argument, because matters of faith, though
they never contradict reason, do transcend it; and Abelard
fell into error rather as Arius had done when he argued
backwards from human fatherhood to its Divine prototype. But his lecture-room was none the less the birthplace of the University of Paris.

In the next century, some other works of Aristotle were
discovered, dealing with the Greek view of natural science;
and the Italian Dominican, Thomas Aquinas, who had a
far more balanced intellect than Abelard, set out to effect
a synthesis between the truths of science as he understood
them, and the truths of revelation. One of the chief

questions which exercised his mind was the *manner* of Our Lord's Presence in the Eucharist. There was no oecumenical pronouncement on the subject, and some sort of definition was rendered very necessary by the crude materialising notions of the Age. Taking the word *substantia*, as Nicaea had taken the equivalent *ousia*, in its philosophical sense of underlying though invisible reality, S. Thomas developed the doctrine of the Real Presence as Transubstantiation, meaning that after consecration the substance or *res* conveyed by the *signum* or sacrament of bread and wine is the glorified Humanity of Jesus. His teaching stimulated devotion to the Blessed Sacrament all over the West, and the Feast of Corpus Christi was instituted in order to give scope for that joy in the homely, heavenly Mystery which on Maundy Thursday is overshadowed by the Cross. We in England see the fruits of this in our Churches. Just as in the earlier centuries unlettered men had put into their music verities that they were not competent to express in words, so now the quickened faith was written in stone. There is an example in Worcestershire, a fragment of an Abbey. Its exquisite arcade, contemporary with S. Thomas, curves gently at the East end as though to bend sheltering arms about the Altar. Above it rises in breathless beauty a roof of the next century, vastly complex yet divinely simple, for every line is perfect and there is a single thought behind it. There are forty-one bosses, all different, each superbly carved to the depth of a man's wrist, though no eye but the angels' can see into them up there. The greatest boss of all looks right down on the Altar, and to it every line leads. Here is a treatise on the Real Presence that anyone can read, a perfect and unceasing act of adoration, a glimpse of the *in*side of Church History—thank God for it.

Concurrently with all these directly religious developments there was a movement towards secular culture in the Middle Ages, scarcely less influential than they upon the life of the Church.   It was in Italy, where the memory of imperial Rome was greenest, that it began.   The *lingua franca* of the educated had all along been a debased form of Latin; from that, once minds began to waken, it was a short step to its classical parent and the forgotten glories of Latin literature.   Reading inspired writing, and so came Dante, Petrarch and Boccaccio, and through them our own Chaucer.   Universities also sprang up like mushrooms, and in one of them, Bologna, the chief study was Roman Civil Law.   From this the interest spread to Canon Law.

Canon Law, the self-ordained legislation of the Church, is of three kinds.   There are Canons proper or the enactments of Councils, there are decrees or judicial pronouncements of Church authorities set forth on their own motion, and there are Decretals or judicial replies of such authorities to questions submitted to them.   The Oecumenical Councils had furnished a body of Canons which was known and accepted everywhere; but beyond that each Church had a collection of Canon Law, issuing from local Councils and authorities, which was more or less peculiar to itself. In the middle of the ninth century, however, an anonymous but resourceful person who wished to back up his bishop against a pushful secular overlord, had drawn up a collection of Canon Law based on an old Spanish one, which in its turn was derived from one made in North Africa in the fifth century.   To this he added out of his own head a series of letters from Popes of the second to fourth centuries *in support of existing episcopal rights*.   In so doing he was no more a forger by the standard of his own times than is the child who for her history preparation writes a letter from Stephen Langton to King John.   He was sure that such letters had once existed and therefore, like the author of the letter of Judas in I Maccabees, felt himself perfectly justified in reconstructing them.   Similarly, following the principle of the Jewish apocalyptists, he put the whole collection under the name of someone to whom it might reasonably be credited,—namely a learned Spanish bishop called Isidore; and nobody ever questioned either the authorship or the authenticity of the Papal letters. When the Law revival set in, in the twelfth century, a monk of Bologna named Gratian incorporated these Pseudo-Isidorian Decretals into a fresh collection, which gained widespread acceptance. Several later Popes, approving such early testimony to their supreme authority, issued editions of Gratian's work under their own names; and so by imperceptible stages Canon Law itself came to be regarded as belonging to the Pope very much as the Bible belongs to the Church. It was a powerful weapon in his armoury and a strong support to his claims. Had he but known it, however, the Isidorian section was to prove eventually for part of Christendom quite a long nail in the said claims' coffin.

The need of Law in the Middle Ages was so great and the search for it so fervent that its thought-forms invaded territory to which they did not properly belong. Mediaeval theologians like S. Anselm took a legalistic view of the Atonement. Instead of regarding it as primarily the Act of God Himself, they represented the Father as an offended Being, Whose wrath against humanity is turned aside by the satisfaction made to Him by Christ as man,—a view which, if followed to its logical conclusion, denies the Unity in the Trinity, for besides obscuring the Divine character of love, it portulates a difference of will between the Persons. But this was not obvious to those who advanced it.

Meanwhile, the man in the street was even more hampered by the limitations of language and outlook than his mental elders. For him, life was a long, laborious effort to scrape up enough merit to take him ultimately to heaven, his notion of hell, the alternative, being luridly unattractive. To this end he performed penances,—or paid someone else to do them for him,—made offerings to the saints, endowed churches and paid in advance for masses for his soul. Poor soul, you say, so limited. But is it so? Anyhow he was clear that sin matters and that the end of man is fellowship with God. And limitation itself, *thlipsis*, all the results of sin, are they not the weapons reft from the Strong, with which the Stronger in His mystical Body is accomplishing the Restoration? It is all right: even in the Middle Ages and even now, the Way of Holiness, the Way hedged in, leads through the wilderness to the New Jerusalem.

CHAPTER XXI

THE CHRISTIAN CHURCH

(v) The Great Awakening in Europe

VIEWED from the standpoint of the present day, the neighbourhood of the year 1500 in Western Europe appears like the sudden eruption of a cork from a bottle, the noise of whose escape, like the crash of Rome's fall, rings yet. Actually, of course, what happened then was the result of movements long stirring,—we saw in the last chapter something of the increasing aeration of the bottle's contents; and the principal events were not simultaneous but spread over some seventy years. Still, people born about 1440 saw a good bit of life before they died in 1520 or so; for within that period the centre of the civilised world shifted with the discovery of America from the Mediterranean seaboard to the Atlantic, the Italian Renaissance came in like a flood, the art of printing was discovered, and Martin Luther defied the Pope and led off half Europe in his train. All of which has a great deal to do with Church History and needs to be more closely examined.

The revival of interest in the classic splendour of ancient Rome had begun, as was natural, in Italy. It was equally natural that the interest should spread to the parent glory of Greece, and that in sympathetic Italy the Greek-speaking scholars of Constantinople, fleeing from the Turk in 1453, should seek shelter for themselves and their precious manuscripts. There is and always has been something intoxicating about Greek; and as in the second century B.C. it had gone to the heads of the High Priests, so now it went to the heads of the Popes. That is why the Vatican is still one of the finest classical museums in the world; that also is why the present Cathedral of S. Peter at Rome is a Renaissance building, the largest Church in the world, and not, as formerly, a fourth-century basilica.

It is rather hard on S. Peter that his Church should have caused so much trouble. The spiritual quality of his successors at this time was not high, and the general trend of the Renaissance south of the Alps, though extremely exciting and delightful, was quite frankly pagan. The idea of building a new S. Peter's was conceived more for the adornment of the Papacy than for the glory of God; and the means adopted for carrying it out were on a par with its motive.

Reference has already been made to the characteristic mediaeval doctrine of Justification by Works; and such a perversion of the truth of God's 'free bounty' through Christ could not issue otherwise than in faulty practice. The Church had always rightly taught that though the *guilt* of sin is forgiven through the Sacraments, the penitent must still do penance, that is undergo punishment for his sin both in proof of the sincerity of his repentance and as a means to spiritual growth. But in practice these penances, which were often very severe, like twenty years on bread and water or a long pilgrimage on foot to a holy place, were frequently evaded: either the penitent paid someone else to do at least part of it for him, or else he paid the authority who imposed it to let him off. In this latter case he received a letter certifying that it was all right, and that letter was called an Indulgence. As temporal punishment was regarded as including the Purgative state after death, the sale of Indulgences had two evil effects; it encouraged the ignorant to think that they could be as wicked as they liked in this world, provided that they or their friends for them bought enough Indulgences to ensure their comfort in the next; and it encouraged unscrupulous and impecunious ecclesiastics to twist their people's tails. To this time-honoured but un-Christian device for raising funds the Vicar of Christ resorted for the new S. Peter's.

Indulgences were not new, nor was objection to them; but hitherto the few consciences that had squirmed had been effectually trampled beneath the heavy foot of custom. Now a new situation arose. North of the Alps the Renaissance took a more serious turn. The Germans were as a race less emotional than the Italians; and, shocked at the latter's pagan licence, they used their new-found Greek not on the classics but on the New Testament. To discover the Gospel for yourself in the original tongue is as inebriating an experience as anyone can desire, and the Germans drank deep of it. Incidentally they did not find anything in the New Testament about Indulgences nor anything much about the Pope; and as they anyhow disliked being mulcted for a Church they would never see and were always imperial rather than papal in their sympathies, this discovery was as welcome as it was surprising. And in making it and kindred matters known, they had the whip-hand of their Italian brethren, in that Germany was the home of the printing-press.

Once the lid is off the petrol-tank, it is only a matter of time before the fumes meet flame and the whole thing blows up. The flame was provided in this case by Martin Luther, Augustinian friar and, at the outset, most sincere and courageous Christian. He said what he thought, was rebuked and bidden to Rome; refused, remembering Huss who under like circumstances had travelled on a safe conduct to the stake; was excommunicated by the Holy See, and publicly destroyed the Bull of Excommunication.

Then the Most Christian Emperor declared him outlaw, and Luther, outlawed and excommunicated, became the popular idol, which, as in the case of Mohammed, resulted in the coarsening of his character and aims. But the Reform movement which he had started was already beyond his control.

It seems to be a condition of our fallen state that we can do nothing without overdoing it. Luther, protesting at first against real evils and repulsed by the supreme authority to which he appealed, went on to protest not only against that authority but against the whole hierarchy which underlay it; and those who followed him out-Luthered Luther to the nth degree.

The consequence was that a large proportion of northern Christendom split off into a multitude of sects, each protesting morning, noon and night about something and at each other, but all alike in three respects, that they preferred to discard rather than to purify abused institutions and doctrines, such as the Apostolic ministry and the Real Presence; that they insisted on the supreme authority of the Bible as interpreted by themselves without reference to tradition; and that some form of the doctrine of Justification by Faith was the central feature in their teaching.

There are periods in history, as there are times in life, which make you feel as though you were shut up in a windowless room with God on the wrong side of the door. Such is the period of the Religious Wars and persecutions which followed the Continental Reformation. It is a mercy really that we do feel like that, for it is the witness in ourselves to the fact that we were made for God and can only be miserable without Him; but it is a false instinct which makes us either roar at our prison-house as at the walls of Jericho, or shrink from facing its acute reality. The key to the door is the statement of fact which Our Lord made at the Ascension: 'Lo, *I am with you* all the days even unto the end of the age,'—that is, of these Last Days.   It is *in* the prison that you are to find Him, not outside, and when you find Him it is no longer a prison but the spacious realm of God.   He who liveth and was dead is *always* walking in the midst of His Church, filling up in her that which is still lacking of His perfect Passion.   So on the scaffold or at the stake, in the dungeon or on the stark and terrible battlefields of the Thirty Years War, when half the people who died never knew what they were fighting for, there was Jesus with His own, like the Fourth who was with the three in the story of the fiery furnace.   Only in the light of this fact can history be sanely read; and it is the more important to read this period sanely, because its happenings are quite literally within earshot of our own times.   Here is a concrete proof of it.   The writer's father, born in 1853, talked at the age of twenty-five to one John Stokes, of Bewdley, in Worcestershire, who was then past ninety.   This old man told him that as a boy he had often heard from an old woman then living how on 3rd September, 1651, her grandfather had stood on Stagborough hill, between Bewdley and Stourport, watching the smoke and hearing the din of the Battle of Worcester, and had seen the fugitive Scots go by, pursued by cavalry.   She had herself heard him tell the tale.   Worcester fight was but three years after the Peace of Westphalia ended the Thirty Years War and established religious toleration on the Continent: yet there was only one life between that battle's ear-witness and the man who was still living in 1878.   Far more than we realise it, the influences from those turbulent days pervade our life.   Where our fathers judged, often at cost of liberty or life, we cheaply prejudge, and, child-like, take a black-and-white view of the Reformation period which is inevitably unjust.   Such prejudices are potent factors in perpetuating our present divisions; and only love's twin offspring, the precious senses of humour and proportion, coupled with the faith that believes *in* man because it believes *in* God Who made him, can open our eyes to the sincerity and courage which on both sides went with both bigotry and vision, and make us peacefully thankful that both we and our fathers have still eternity in which to know the truth.

Yet it is true none the less that, had the Church been anything but a Divine institution, abidingly indwelt by the living and most patient Spirit, she would have been more dead than any doornail by the seventeenth century. Instead of which she rose to new life. It is a relief to turn back from the religious wars, which went on till 1648, to the Counter-Reformation, which began a century earlier and went on concurrently with them.

The seven thousand who had not bowed the knee to Baal, or having bowed, had repented of their infidelity, were by no means confined to Germany, nor were Elijahs lacking within the pale of Rome. But the Papal prophets fought with different weapons, and it is instructive to notice what they were.

At about the same time that Luther was pinning his ninety-five theses to the door of the Castle Church at Wittenberg, some sixty priests in Rome, acting on the principle of 'reform yourself first,' were banding together into a society without vows, known as the Oratory of Divine Love, to revive spiritual life and the dignity of worship. Their numbers increased, and some years later a discerning Pope made six of them Cardinals; and these drew up at his bidding a programme of reform, in which they not only denounced the evils in the Church as fervidly as any Protestant, but also pointed the remedy. The root of all was clerical corruption from the Papacy downwards; so simony, nepotism and pluralism must cease, and steps be taken to provide a moral and instructed clergy and a reformed body of Religious. *And it happened.* Faith and obedience brought their blessing. It is lovely history to read, this Valley-of-Dry-Bones revival in the sixteenth century. Old Orders were reformed and new ones founded by great leaders to meet the present need. S. Philip Neri founded the Congregation of the Oratory for clergy and laity alike, and thereby wrought a miracle of cleansing in the Augean stable of Renaissance Rome. Communities both of men and women were formed on a new principle, combining the life of the cloister with active work in the care of the sick, the sinful and the ignorant. Most influential of all these was the Society of Jesus, founded in 1540 by the Spaniard Ignatius Loyola. Its primary object was to combat heresy and ignorance by sound teaching,—a new thing, this, for hitherto no one had preached except the friars. The Jesuits were splendidly trained and gloriously believing and obedient. They went wherever the Pope sent them, and by their agency not only was a great part of Europe recovered for Catholicism but missions were planted in countries of the Far East hitherto unevangelised. Francis Xavier is the saint chiefly associated with these; and it is worth noting that his hymn, 'My God, I love Thee,' exactly expresses the Christian ideal of loving response to the infinite bounty which was obscured equally by the mediaeval insistence on works and by the Lutheran overstress on faith. It is a comfort when for once somebody hits a happy medium.

While all these things were happening, the Emperor Charles V was planning for reform in another direction. This imperial Elijah was quite determined that matters needing reform should be brought before a Council; and as soon as the cessation of his French wars left him free to put his utmost pressure on the Pope, he got his way. The Council met at Trent in 1545 and with long intervals of inactivity concluded its business in 1563. On the doctrinal side, it drew up plain statements of traditional belief on the three subjects, hitherto undefined, which were most called in question by the Protestants,—namely, Authority, Justification and the manner of the Eucharistic Presence. In regard to the first, Scripture and the traditions of faith and practice received '*quasi per manus*' from the earliest times were said to constitute *together* the Church's source of authority; and it was pointed out that the Creed of Nicaea derived equally from both. Justification was defined as translation from the fallen state, in which all the sons of Adam are born, into the state of grace and sonship to God through Jesus the Second Adam. As this involves not only forgiveness of sins but also the progressive sanctification of the whole man by correspondence with the grace received, faith appears as the *beginning* of Justification but not the whole of it; the constant co-operation of the will is necessary also. Against the minimising and destructive views of the Protestants, both the Sacrificial reality of the Eucharist and the doctrines of Transubstantiation in the philosophical sense were affirmed. It was pointed out also that this Real Presence of Christ in His Sacrament is in no way incompatible with His heavenly Presence; and further that the Eucharist differs from other Sacraments in that it has *three* parts instead of two,—the *res* or thing signified by the outward sign or *sacramentum* of bread and wine, namely the Body and Blood of Christ, being distinct from the *virtus* or benefit received, and having therefore a sanctity *independent of reception*. Which same threefold distinction you will find, if you look, in our quite independent Church Catechism!

In practical reform the greatest work of the Council was the establishment of seminaries for training the clergy. The question of Papal supremacy was not discussed; but as everything was referred to the Pope's approval, the position so long claimed was secured, though without definition. Well, we may not agree about the claim, but we can love and admire the great Catholic and Apostolic

Church of Rome, which from the manifold denials of the Middle Ages came thus in the fifteenth century to a 'change of mind' almost as great as Peter's own.

CHAPTER XXII

THE CHRISTIAN CHURCH

(vi) The Church in England from the Reformation to the Present Day

ENGLISH Church History is receiving a chapter to itself, because if this book has any readers, they will presumably be English people whose primary concern with the past is to trace in it the roots of their own present. In any case you would have to consider the English Reformation by itself, for the course it took was in many ways unique.

There is a good deal to be said for being an island as well as an independent monarchy. Owing to these two circumstances this country which, when the Reformation began, was just settling down to a new and prosperous era under the Tudors, escaped the religious wars which devastated Germany and France. She did not, however, escape either the Reformation or the Renaissance which gave it birth; but her island blood took both more mildly and turned them to rather different account.

In 1631, Latin was still the *lingua franca* of the educated, and both the New Learning and the new theology had in it crossed the channel. But the breach with Rome was not effected here by any movement of popular desire: it was chiefly the work of the potentate upon whom, a few years before the Pope had bestowed the title Defender of the Faith for writing a book against Luther. Now Pope met Pope, and it was the royal Pope who won. Failing to obtain the consent of the Holy See to his divorce from Katharine of Aragon, Henry VIII declared *himself* the Supreme Head of the Church in England; and when excommunicated by the Pope took no notice. You cannot justify his demand for divorce, nor his subsequent action, nor the Pope's reply: both acted wrongly, but there it is. And the immediate result was of course to divide England into two camps, respectively royal and papal in their sympathies; and also to make her a Cave of Adullam for Continental Protestants whose own countries were too hot to hold them.

The despotic and much-marrying Henry did not, however, make any change in the age-old constitution of the Church. Though he rid this country of the trammels of Papal supremacy in order to bind it with his own, there was no break in the Apostolical Succession nor in any other fundamental Catholic tradition. The schism was of the same nature as that between East and West five centuries before. In terms of the ship illustration, it was a further division of decks within the ship, whereby Ecclesia Anglicana found herself the middle of three, on speaking terms with neither neighbour; it was *not*, as in the case of the Continental Protestants, a taking to the boats. Nevertheless the occupants of the middle deck after the schism fraternised considerably with the occupants of the flotilla alongside.

The Defender of the Faith was not a person to brook opposition, or to acquiesce in shortness of purse; and the English Religious communities, besides being upholders of the Papal supremacy against his own, were also principal landowners. Them therefore, by methods as reprehensible as his motives, Henry proceeded to dissolve, and sucked thereout no small advantage in material wealth. The Religious were, however, pensioned after a fashion, and to the infinite disgust of the extreme Protestants, forbidden under pain of death to break their vow of chastity! As you look at the maimed and roofless ruins which witness still to the tragedy that was being enacted there just over four hundred years ago, your heart bleeds or exults according to your predisposition. But reasonable Christianity requires a more temperate view. The Religious Life is of the Spirit, integral to the Church and indestructible; but the temporal forms in which it is contained grow at times too narrow for its spirit, and it passes under the common law of death as the road to life. In the sixteenth century in England it had served its turn, and its disappearance created, among other things, a problem of Poor Relief which is not yet fully solved. But *as it then was*, it could not have met the needs of the new age. So by the over-ruling providence of God it fell into the ground and in the sight of the unwise seemed to die; then after three centuries it rose and began in our own times to bring forth much fruit. Which was far better in the long run than abiding above-ground alone.

Henry, in this respect Defender of the Faith in spite of himself, had already before the schism done it more deliberate service by ordering a copy of the English Bible to be placed in every church. This was followed in 1549, two years after the accession of his young son Edward VI, by the first English Prayerbook, which was a far greater innovation. Picture that Whitsunday in any old church that you know, for those walls witnessed it. For the first time in history, not the epistle and gospel only but the whole of the Eucharist 'commonly called the Mass,' was rendered in our mother-tongue, that ripe and home-grown English whose lovely cadences echo none the less the stately rhythm of the best Latin prose. Nor was it the Mass only that was so rendered. The Monastic Choir Office, which must otherwise have fallen into disuse, became in the simplified form of English Matins and Evensong of daily obligation in all churches.

But the Book of 1549 had a short life. The master-minds among the extreme Reformers, who had not attempted to tackle his father, set to work gaily on young Edward. The letters of the period make you laugh, though they also make you very glad you did not live in it. There was a Swiss called Bullinger in particular, whom half the devout notables in England seem to have held in more than Papal reverence. He and his ilk bombarded the boy-king with treatises and sermons,—the appetite of the day for sermons was insatiable. They called him Josiah, which implied that his father had been Amon and Manasseh; and the result of all this was the Second Prayerbook of 1552. They were even planning to hold a great Protestant council in England in opposition to the 'vile birds assembled at Trent,' when to their horror Josiah died, and the tide of extreme Reform was stemmed by five years of bitter perse-cution under his sister Mary, the Papist daughter of the divorced Katharine, who alone of the Tudors had no understanding of her people. She married Philip of Spain in the year following her accession, and the Reformers, who derived much of their vocabulary as well as their theology from the Old Testament, relieved their feelings by calling them Ahab and Jezebel. In view of all these happenings within ten years, just imagine the Scylla and Charybdis situation which faced the twenty-five year old Elizabeth on her accession in 1558.

Elizabeth had retained her head on her shoulders up to that date only by keeping her own religious views undiscoverable. She had all her father's love of power and of national independence, but she had not her sister's persecuting spirit. With all her faults she loved and understood her people; and for her settlement of the Church question we owe her a debt which it is easy to underestimate.

First, she discreetly changed her royal title from Supreme Head of the Church to Supreme *Governor*, which implied only the right to administer existing laws. Then she caused the issue of an Act of Uniformity, which made the revised Prayerbook of 1559 the only legal service-book and imposed a fine on all who failed to attend Church on Sunday; a measure which ruled out on the one hand the Roman Catholics and on the other the extreme Reformers or Independents, but included all sorts in between. Twelve years later appeared the Thirty Nine Articles of Religion, which your new vicar still reads to you on the first Sunday after his induction. Most people nowadays, reading them only at face value, hate the Articles; but they are really quite a gallant attempt to strike the happy medium of genuine Catholicity between debased Romanism and extreme Reform; and if you interpret their language in relation to the thought of the age which produced it, it is by no means impossible to square them with the contemporary pronouncements of Trent. It is easy of course to deplore the losses consequent on the Elizabethan Settlement; yet by its means the Church of England became a real *via media*, retaining all the essentials of Catholicity and with singular freedom for development. And who that ever sat on mortal throne could under the circumstances have done it better?

For the most unfortunate feature of Elizabeth's reign the person most to blame was not the Queen but the Pope. In 1570, he took upon himself to declare her deposed, and as that at once made all Roman Catholics potential traitors, 'Popery' came to be regarded in England as the deadly foe of national liberty. Under the Stuarts who followed her there was a still further confusion of issues religious and political. Despotic monarchy came to go with episcopacy, and the rights of Parliament with that dour but disciplined variety of dissent known as Puritanism.

The crisis came in the Civil War, that is not yet three hundred years ago. The Puritans wrecked our churches, but they also gave us *Pilgrim's Progress*, and we should be poorer stuff as a nation to-day had we none of their blood in our veins. Eleven years of their unsmiling rule proved, however, enough for merry England, and the two sons of the murdered Charles were recalled to sit in turn on their father's throne. Of these, James II crowned a lifetime of *faux pas* by producing at the eleventh hour an inconvenient and Roman Catholic son. James was thereupon deftly and bloodlessly exchanged by his subjects for his nephew and son-in-law, the Protestant William of Orange.

Having thus after much pains secured a constitutionally-minded monarch, the English people reached two great decisions: first, that religious toleration must be established; and second, that nobody must ever again be allowed to interfere with national institutions. In regard to the first, the Continental countries had already set the example: we, following later, unfortunately went on to think that what one believes does not really matter. In regard to the second, you can hardly blame the generation that had experienced three Stuarts in succession for wanting a bit of peace; but it was an unfortunate conclusion, because it carried with it the belief that whatever is, is right, which proved later so stubborn a barrier to reform not only in Church affairs but also in such matters as the rotten boroughs and the Slave Trade. The Eighteenth Century is a sad time. You should not read about it unless you have caught from God something of the infinite pity which alone suffices for the pathos of human life.

On both sides of the Channel, people were worn out with their fathers' experience in the last two centuries; and like the victims of an ultra-violent spring-cleaning they

lay down on the bare boards and slept.   So the fool said
in his weary heart, 'There is no God,' and his neighbour
answered, 'No, and if there is, He does not care.'   Poor
fools!   Who has not read their epitaphs and wept for
the dulness of the lives that, lacking the vision of God,
could leave behind a record of such unimprovable perfection?

But there was another side.   Institutions were not to
be tampered with, and the Church, mercifully, has been
institutional from birth.   So, though bishops were plur-
alists, clergy indifferent and everybody uninstructed, the
Sacraments, which are the safeguards of the Church's
Catholicity, continued to be validly, if infrequently,
administered.

And there was always a faithful remnant.

'I will be as the dew upon Israel,' said God to Hosea.
As then, so now.   In 1729 William Law, greatly believing,
published his 'Serious Call to a Devout and Holy Life.'
In the same year the Wesley brothers began to emulate
at Oxford the ordered life of the early Church, which pro-
cedure earned them from their amazed beholders the title
of Methodists.   Some years later, the Wesleys met some
German Moravians and through their influence came to
attach a paramount importance to sudden, emotional conversion.   This brought in its wake some perversions of
doctrine, but the movement was Catholic in its inception
and from the first intensely missionary.   It brought vital
religion to the spiritually starved lower classes, especially
in the new industrial districts.   But alas! the official
Church, blind and self-satisfied like Laodicea, had no use
for what she called 'enthusiasm,'* and a quarter of her
members were driven into schism.   Another boat added
to the flotilla, a further weakening of the corporate
efficiency of the Body of Christ.   It was a tragic pity, but,

* The equivalent of fanaticism in eighteenth-century parlance

thank God, the boats were still the *Ship's* boats and all are on the same course.

A century later, another Revival movement awoke within the Church, which, like the Counter-Reformation three centuries earlier, stayed within its Apostolic borders. The Rationalists of the eighteenth century considered it silly to believe in anything, whether ghost, ideal or God, which you could not see, and held that this was a tidy, tangible world wound up to go on for ever just the same. Then came the French Revolution, which was not tidy at all, and reaction set in. Thus was born Romanticism, which thawed the icebound faculty of wonder and so, despite its extravagances, reopened the way to faith. It blossomed in literature and in our own country took two directions. Wordsworth saw God in nature, and Scott saw thrills in mediaeval Catholicism, and with amazing penetration joined the English Church as the nearest thing available to it. Their influence reached in his country rectory John Keble, a young man bred in the best traditions of the faithful remnant, and moved him to write for his own relief romantic poems on the Christian Year. The collection, published at his father's wish, fell like rain on the mown grass, and went through ninety-seven editions in the author's life-time. A few years later, Keble with three other Fellows of Oriel, Froude, Newman and Pusey, began that Valley-of-Dry-Bones revival which is known variously as the Oxford Movement from its birthplace, the Tractarian from its method of propaganda and the Catholic from the direction which it took.

Equally with the Methodists, the Tractarians laid stress upon holiness as an essential mark of the Church; unlike them, they stressed also the importance of the Apostolical Succession as the safeguard of continuity, and strove by appeal to the faith and practice of the first five centuries to restore to living use the neglected elements of Catholicism inherent in our formularies. They began to do this only a hundred years ago, within our fathers' memory, and how great things the Lord has done for us already, whereof we rejoice!

So here we are, at our own day. The Ship of Pentecost is trawling still, and we, hands on her middle deck, look out over the uncharted ocean ahead, *expecting*.

CHAPTER XXIII

THE UNFULFILLED PROPHECIES OF THE CONSUMMATION

THE things which we are expecting are matters of faith. Where the Jews looked for Redemption and believed that it would come, because God Who is the Truth Dependable had promised it, *we* for whom Redemption is a matter of past fact and present experience, look still for its consummation. And that consummation, so far as it can be specified, consists in the Second Coming of that same Jesus Whom in A.D. 29 a cloud received from the Apostles' sight, the Resurrection of the Body, the Judgment of living and dead, and the Life of the Age to come.

It would be an interesting study to go through the Bible after the manner of the author of Hebrews, only in greater detail, marking in red ink every place where, explicitly or otherwise, *faith* emerges as the central thing that matters. One might then go through History in the same way, noting how progress has always been through the seed of Abraham, people like Paul, Athanasius, Gregory, Francis, Ignatius Loyola, Philip Neri, Wesley and Keble, who believed *in* God and acted accordingly. In so doing, you would see fulfilment following faith in every case; but you would also see that no fulfilment has ever yet been complete. The Old Testament prophecies of a glorious future were only very partially fulfilled by the Return and Restoration: even the Incarnation was only potentially complete. The Eternal Word has assumed our nature in His own Person, and in it has spoken the *Tetelestai*. But the purpose of Creation will not be perfectly fulfilled until He has clothed Himself with all humanity, and in it has spoken again that golden word. The subjects of the Unfulfilled Prophecies are, therefore, integral to the Christian creed: without them the historical statements about Creation and Redemption are like an unfinished sentence, meaningless. If you want to see the Wood as a whole, you must not leave out these Trees, for they are the avenue that leads beyond its shadows to the City of God.

So put away the thronging present, and be brave. Do not think of these Last Days as a road winding endlessly uphill until it is lost to sight on the horizon, for that is discouraging. Think of them rather as a circle steadily closing in upon its centre, the whole vast circumference pulsing with Expectation. We on earth may be sluggish about that, but no one else is. The whole of humanity beyond the veil is expecting, and so is the Ascended Lord. Even on the Cross His eyes were on that central point, and for that joy set before Him He endured.

The prophecies do not, of course, give us a complete picture. They deal with realities beyond our present experience, which, even when they are put across to us in metaphor from familiar things, we can only very dimly apprehend. Their demand on faith is insistent. But after all, it is easier for us than it was for Abraham. His faith in God's promises soared straight up into the blue without previous experience of His Truth: we have four thousand years of revelation behind us. Moreover, the prophecies are all of a piece with what we already know. Take the Second Coming. Like everything that is perfect, it is paradoxical. It appears as both sudden and fore-warned. But the signs of the Coming are such as only believers can read: the life-story of the Church follows that of her Head, and it is again the darkest hour that comes before the dawn. Over and over again you get this. 'When the Son of Man cometh, shall He find faith on the earth?' says Our Lord. Yes, indeed, faith in its highest and hardest form, the agony of the Fourth Word that brings to birth the triumph of the Sixth. The apostolic writers develop this thought, and see the power of evil culminate in the person of an Antichrist; in the Apocalypse this appears further as a sort of Satanic parody of the Incarnation and the Church. The fact that, as S. John of the Epistle points out, there have already been many antichrists in a limited sense, types of the final Antichrist as there were types of Christ, in no way lessens the force of what all the prophecies declare, that the evil in the world has got to come to a head in some supremely terrible form, in order that the returning Christ may manifest at last the supreme completeness of His victory over it. In His Mystical Body, as once in That which He took of Mary, the Word of God will pass and even now *is* passing through death to life and through defeat to unimaginable victory, destroying the Strong One with his own weapons. Therefore, 'When these things begin to come to pass, look up and lift up your heads,'—giving thanks for them as the Lord did in the same night in which He was betrayed,— 'for your redemption draweth nigh.'

The Coming itself is paradoxical in another way. The word *parousia*, which is commonly used for it, really means not coming but *Presence*. It is also spoken of as the *apokalupsis* or revelation of the Lord and as the *epiphaneia* or manifestation of His presence,—*parousia* again. Quite clearly, the Second Advent is not the return of One long absent, but the showing or unveiling of the Ever-Presence which is now hidden. 'The consummation of the age,' of which He spoke, *is* His Second Coming, which will end these Last Days and inaugurate a new era.

The Coming issues in the Resurrection, and on the Resurrection follows Judgment.

The teaching of Our Lord in the Fourth Gospel is that bodily resurrection belongs to man only as a result of the

Incarnation, and further that for believers Resurrection is the outcome of Regeneration, the result of that union with the Incarnate Word, of which the Eucharist is both means and pledge.

S. Paul, who sees the resurrection of 'the dead in Christ' as accompanying the Second Coming and followed by the rapture of the living saints into the same state, develops this teaching in regard to the members of the Second Adam by means of the analogy of the corn. You sow in your field hard, dry grain. It falls into the earth, is covered and disintegrated; but in the spring the germ of life which had persisted expresses itself in a new form,—the fresh green plant. Just as a person, who was familiar with grain but had never seen a green cornfield, could never guess that the one would result from the other, so there is a surprise beyond all imagining in store for us when the Lord, in the Springtime of His Return, clothes the world in the glory of the Resurrection. The principle is 'to every seed his own body'; so for the faithful soul the risen body will be the perfect expression, instrument and outcome of himself, no longer in any way a burden or a hindrance.

We get still further light on the nature and properties of our butterfly stage in its ultimate perfection from the narratives of those Forty Days in A.D. 29, when in it Our Lord was seen and touched on earth. The thing supremely clear is that for all its glorious difference, its freedom from the laws of time and space as we understand them, the Risen Body of Jesus was *the same* as that in which He died; for the existence of the new involved both the disappearance of the old and the persistence of its supreme characteristics. It is baffling, of course, and on our present knowledge inexplicable; but it is stamped with reality, with ultimate, satisfying truth all over. And Nature shouts it at you on every side. If familiarity has blunted for you the joyful mystery of spring, go to a dewpond on the downs in May,—on Ascension Day, it may be, when

the sky is blue as when the Lord went up, and the clouds
are having a dress-rehearsal for His Coming Again, and
see the dragon-fly nymphs, brown and ugly, crawl from the
muddy water which is their native element, and cling
expectant to the reeds. Watch them, as the sun kisses
them, give birth to their new selves, exquisite, iridescent,
unbelievably free; and know that it doth not yet appear
what *we* shall be. The Incarnate Word, from Whom the
created order takes its being, has already raised it in His
own Person to its highest plane and power. Not only
does the universe still belong to Him, but He, as Man,
still belongs to the universe. For all our modern science
and our Higher Criticism, we are but babes as yet, spelling
out the first page in the joint volume of Revelation and
Discovery. But surely when we have read further, we
shall understand the Resurrection, the Transfiguration,
the Real Presence and all the other mysteries of super-
nature in terms of laws which are no less divine and
adorable for being truly natural.

One other point calls for comment in this context.
There is in the Apocalypse one passage which seems to
distinguish *two* resurrections as separate events in time.
S. John speaks of the blessedness of the martyrs and con-
fessors who have part in the first resurrection, because
over them the second death has no power, and after it
they will reign with Christ for a thousand years before the
rest of the dead live at all. During that period Satan will
be bound, but at its close he will be loosed. On his
loosing follow his final overthrow and the Last Judgment.

The idea of the Millennium or Thousand Years was
borrowed by S. John from the Jewish apocalypses; and
the literate interpretation put upon it by many in early
times almost resulted in the exclusion of his book from the
Canon, for it was felt that belief in a visible and undisturbed
reign of Our Lord with the risen Saints on earth *between*
His Second Coming and the Final Judgment was at

variance with the other teaching of Scripture, which shows the Church as suffering right up to the end. A more fruitful line of interpretation was first suggested by S. Augustine of Hippo. He took the first resurrection as meaning that true share in Our Lord's own which is given to believers in Baptism, and the binding of Satan, which recalls at once the figure of the Stronger and the Strong, as Our Lord's conquest of him on the Cross. The Millennium thus becomes the present age, the period between the two Advents in which the eternal completeness of the Redemption once effected is being worked out, and the unloosing of Satan at its close as that final ebullition of evil, elsewhere foretold, which results first in the seeming destruction of the Church and then in the actual destruction of itself. This interpretation is borne out by the number 1,000, which, symbolic like all the numbers in the Apocalypse, signifies the perfection of God's work. It also helps one to see what our Catechism means by saying that the baptised are not heirs merely, but actually *inheritors* of the Kingdom of Heaven. It is, in part, ours already. We do really and truly reign with Christ on earth *now*. The Millennium may of course mean much more than this, something at which we cannot guess; but this way of looking at it, consonant as it is with the rest of Scripture, can hardly be otherwise than right as far as it goes. There is no confusion between the resurrections. From among the myriads who had predeceased Him, Jesus the Second Adam rose, nineteen centuries ago, alone. All who subsequently have been or will be united to Him in His Mystical Body are, while yet in their mortal bodies, sharers both in His death and in His Resurrection: the body that shall be is being mysteriously prepared in them as the perfect creature is prepared within the larva or the plant within the seed. At the Parousia this hidden process will be openly fulfilled, alike in the dead and in the living, and on the Resurrection follows Judgment.

The Final Judgment appears as the immediate purpose and effect of the Second Coming. Just as the Parousia is the open showing of Our Lord's now hidden Presence, so is the Judgment the manifestation of *reality* in regard to every individual soul. It is the flood-lighting of the world, and Jesus is the Judge because He is both the Light that floods and the Standard in relation to which all values are henceforth seen. The mediaeval mind saw the Judgment as a law-court, where sinners pled in anguish before the bar, and watched with trembling fear to see the scales go down. But the teaching of Scripture is that the judgment is *self-determined*, that the thing which settles it is love and that the light which makes it manifest is Love. It is no less terrible for that, but perfectly consonant with all previous revelation. Man was created to express God, and God is Love. Man therefore fulfils the purpose of his creation just in so far as he is loving, and no further. Every life offers scope for love and the love given or refused to fellow-men is given or refused to the Creator-Word Incarnate in Whom alone they are. So when the Son of Man comes in His glory and all the holy angels with Him, there is no hearing of cases, for in His presence the self-determined judgment is evident. It is either 'Come' or 'Depart,' at once.

And now to grasp the fiercest nettle in the whole field of Scripture. How is 'depart' to be reconciled with the perfection of God's love and the completeness of redemption?

Well, let us admit straight away that the matter is a mystery. Like that which preceded it, the revelation given with the First Advent takes us only to the threshold of the new age, and we must wait to learn the rest until we get there. This is not unreasonable. Nobody ever does see the whole road before they start, and it is just that incompleteness of our knowledge which gives scope for faith. And we have really got quite enough to go on with.

Clear-cut as the distinction is between the saved and those whom we somewhat prematurely call the lost, the fact that the Judgment is 'for every man according to his works' implies degrees in the Divine approval or condemnation almost as many as there are individual souls. Our Lord taught the same thing in His explanation of the Parable of the Servants, some of whom were beaten with many stripes and some with few. He said also that the judgment would be 'more tolerable' for the inhabitants of the notorious Cities of the Plain, whom S. Jude describes as 'suffering the punishment of eternal fire,' than for the religious Jews who refused the Gospel. And He told those same Jews that the publicans and harlots would go into the Kingdom of Heaven before them, but He did not say that they themselves would not go in at all. What we are really up against is the question of punishment, and about that two things are perfectly certain. In the first place, any punishment that comes from God comes from love, and must therefore be recreative in purpose and power. It is dwarfing God to our own stature to read into His punishment any of the personal vindictiveness which too often characterises its human counterpart. It is integral to the method of our redemption that pain should be used by Love to purify the beloved, and there is no pain in all the world that hurts so much as seeing oneself against the holiness of God. This pain must result in *all* men in some degree from the Parousia and Judgment. Secondly, like the sorrows that result from sin in this world, this punitive pain depends for its effectiveness on the way in which it is received: there is love's chance again, for it is loving, thankful acceptance which makes it a means of blessing. The phrases 'eternal fire,' 'eternal punishment,' and so forth, need to be read in the light of these facts. Historically, they are the product of the pre-Christian belief that the enemies of God would be punished before the eyes of the righteous in Gehenna, the valley of the Sons of

Hinnom to the south of Jerusalem, which had been the scene in degenerate times of idolatrous human sacrifice; and mediaeval thought, lacking the perfect love that casts out fear, construed them into a material hell of endless torment. But as a matter of fact, the thought in the *locus classicus* of S. Mark about 'Gehenna where their worm dieth not and the fire is not quenched' is not that of torment but of *decay*. The drift of the whole passage is that to refuse the way of the Cross, which leads through death to life, is to develop a spiritual condition comparable to that of corruption in the body,—to pass, that is, through unmortified bodily life to spiritual death. There is, moreover, a tradition that in later times the valley of Hinnom was used as a burying-ground for corpses, a place, that is, for *getting rid* of corruption. It is not known whether this was so in Our Lord's time, but if it were, how close it brings us to the thought of the Parousia and Judgment,—the pain that follows on the vision of Him Whose eyes are as a flame of fire! And anyhow, surely we can trust Our Lord.

There is a story of some Scotch fishermen overtaken in their boat at night by a terrific storm. Amid the din and fury of the elements they lost consciousness; and when they awoke in calm, sunlit waters with a verdant landscape around them, they thought that they had died in the storm and woken in another world. But it was not so. The terrible but temporary violence of wind and waves had swept their boat out of danger into an inland loch; and, saved by a miracle, they were still in their own country.

Here is a faint analogy for the transition at the close of the Apocalypse from the vision of the Loosing of Satan and of the Great White Throne of Judgment to that of the New Jerusalem, the City of God that lies in full sunshine beyond the shadows of the Wood. For in this vision the very storm that sought to wreck the Church has washed her into port: evil has destroyed itself. Yet, though sin and its consequences have entirely disappeared, the scene is still *earth*. The New Humanity, coextensive at last with the whole human race, comes down from her home in heaven to the New Earth that is itself a part of Heaven. The Lord's Prayer is fulfilled; His Kingdom that shall have no end has come at last on earth as it has ever been in heaven. The larval universe that culminates in man has reached its perfect form, and of the created order that now reflects unbroken the threefold Divine Likeness, individual, social and creative, the Slain yet Living Lamb is Centre of worship as He is Source of life. In the New Jerusalem, crowning the New Heaven and Earth, every thought that has served as a staff on our pilgrimage finds its fulfilment. It is Eden where men walk with God and eat of the Tree of Life; it is Bethel, Tabernacle and Temple, and the Building so long and wearily preparing behind the hoarding of history. It is the final issue of the process of turning water into wine; the limitless liberty which issues from the straitened Way; the dawn that follows the last and darkest of all the dark hours of time; the completion of the work of Restoration, of the purpose of Creation and Redemption; the issue of God's age-long and amazing belief in man, and the crown of man's faltering response of faith in Him. Here God has got at last what He has always wanted, and Creation that for which it was created. Free and articulate in man who sums it up, the whole gamut of created things gives itself back to Him Who made it in perfect adoration, believing, loving, obedient and therefore wholly happy.

The vision is almost beyond bearing. In all previous fulfilments there has been an element of disappointment, making room for greater good to come. Now at last the ultimate ideal is reached; fulfilment is absolute and every desire is satisfied. *Yet after all it is only the beginning.* The name of God is still *I will be*, and as the symphony of

Restoration sinks to its final, you perceive that it was only an overture. For the New Jerusalem is but the *Bride* of the Lamb; and when she goes in with Him to the marriage-feast the door is shut, and we have no inkling of what, in the eternal creativeness of love, will issue from their union. We have reached the end of the record of revelation given with the First Advent; but its final, faithful word *AMEN*, that sums up the past, also guarantees the future.

אמן

APPENDIX OF REFERENCES

Suggestive rather than exhaustive.

[The documentary divisions are taken from Driver's *Introduction to the Literature of the O.T.*]

INTRODUCTION TO THE OLD TESTAMENT

Page

5.   Title of prophet applied to Samuel: 1 Sam. iii. 20.
                                           Elijah: Mal. iv. 5.
                                           Abraham: Gen. xx. 7
                                           E.
                                         Moses: Deut. xxxiv. 10.
                                           David: Acts iii, 20.
    Nebhi'im on Carmel: 1 Kings xviii. 19ff.
    Sons of the prophets: 1 Sam. x. 5–13, xix. 23ff, cp. 1 Kings xviii. 3 and 4, 2 Kings ii. 5ff.

8.   Early written sources: Joshua x. 13, 2 Sam. i. 18, Num. xxi. 14, cp. 1 Kings xi. 41.
    Finding of Law-book: 2 Kings xxii. 3ff.

9.   Legal codes: J.   Exod. xxiv. 17–28.
                        E.   Exod. xx.–xxiii.
                        D.   Deut. xii.–xxvi.
                        P.   Chiefly Leviticus, of which Chapters xvii.–xxvi. are the Law of Holiness (H), probably a product of the school of Ezekiel.

CHAPTER III

THE CREATION

Page
12. Creation-story: (1) Gen. i. 1 to ii. 4 (created) P.
      (2) Gen. ii. 4 (In the day . . .) to
      end of chapter.   J.

CHAPTER IV

THE FALL

23. Adam story (continuation of J's creation story),
  Gen. iii.

24. Story of angel marriages: Gen. vi. 1–4.   J.

25. Second-Isaiah on origin of evil: Isa. xlv. 7.
  S. Paul's doctrine of Christ as the Second Adam:
  1 Cor. xv., cp. Rom. v., vi., vii.

28. "Not for our sins only. . . . ": 1 John ii. 2.
  Crown of thorns: S. Mark xv. 17 and parallels.

30. "It doth not yet appear. . . . ": 1 John iii. 2.

CHAPTER V

FROM THE FALL TO THE CALL OF ABRAHAM

31. Pre-history from the Fall to Abraham: Gen. iv. 1
  to xi. 27.
  J: iv., v. 29, vi. 1–8, vii. 1–5, 7–10, 12, 16b, 17b,
  22, 23, viii. 2b, 3a, 6–12, 13b, 20–22, ix. 18–27,
  x. 8–19, 21, 24–30, xi. 1–9.
  P: All the rest.

33f. Life-story of Abraham: Gen. xi. 28 to xxv. 10.
  The story of his call in xii. 1–4 is J, as also
  are the repetitions of the promises to him or his

Page

seed in xviii. 17–19, xxii. 15–18, xxvi. 24, xxviii. 13–16. That in xv. 1–21 is JE, and E appears alone for the first time in Chapter xx.

Chapter xiv., in which Amraphel and Chedor-laomer are mentioned, is the only passage in the book and indeed in the Hexateuch derived from a special source outside J, E, D and P.

CHAPTER VI

FROM ABRAHAM TO MOSES

38ff.   Primitive religion:—

Bethels: Gen. xxviii. 10–22.   Two stories are here beautifully interwoven:—

J: verses 10, 13–16 (read RV margin), 19;
E: „   11, 12, 17, 18, 20–22.

Compare Gen. xii. 6, 7 J, xxxv. 7 E, Judges vi. 11–24, 1 Sam. vi. 14, 15.

Obelisks and pillars: Exod. xxiv. 4 E, Joshua iv. 20, 1 Kings vii. 21, 2 Kings xvii. 10, Hos. iii. 4, 2 Kings xviii. 4, xxiii. 6, Deut. xii. 3 xvi. 21.

Libations: Gen. xxviii. 18 E.

Animal sacrifices: Gen. xv. 9–12 JE, Exod. xxiv. 5–8 E, Num. xxii. 40 to xxiii. 4 E, Judges vi. 19–28, 1 Sam. xi. 15, etc. etc.

Human sacrifice: Gen. xxii. E, Judges xi. 29–40, cp. 2 Kings xvi. 3, xxi. 6.

Probably implied in practice of redeeming the first-born: Exod. xiii. 13, 15 J.

High-places: 1 Kings iii. 2, xii. 31, xxii. 43, etc.

Ritual acts investing slaying of victim with sacrificial significance: Exod. xxiv. 6–8 E, Lev. vi. 24ff, ix. 7–end, xvi, Exod. xii. 7 P, etc.

Sabbath: Exod. xxiii. 12 E, xxxiv. 21 J, cp. 2 Kings iv. 23, Hos. ii. 11, Amos viii. 5; P legislation: Exod. xxxi. 12–17, xxxv. 1–3, Lev. xxiii. 3 (H).

Page

Circumcision: Exod. iv. 22–26 J, Josh. v. 2–9
(verses 2, 3, 8, 9 are JE, verses 4–7 D);
Gen. xvii. 1–14 and Exod. xii. 43ff P.

Food-law, because "the life is in the blood":
Lev. xvii. 10–14 H, cp. iii. 17 P.

43.   The Joseph stories: Gen. xxxvii.–l.
Almost entirely J and E interwoven.
       In Chapter xxxvii. verses 1 and 2 to "Jacob"
are P, then J and E alternate. Note that J has
Ishmaelites and E Midianites as the men to whom
Joseph is sold; in J Judah takes the lead, in
E Reuben.
Israel in Egypt: Exod. i. and ii.
J i. 6, 8–12, ii. 15–23 'died.'
E i. 15 to ii. 14.
P i. 1–5, 7, 13–14.

44ff. Early life and call of Moses (1): Exod. iii. 1 to
vi. 1, alternately J and E; (2) Exod. vi. 2 to
vii. 6 P.
       The narrative of the Plagues, the Passover,
the Exodus and the Crossing of the Red Sea
(vii. 7 to xv. 21) is mostly J and E but the
directions for the Passover are P.
Events of the journey.
       Manna: Exod. xvi. verses 4 and 5, and 25–30
are J, the rest P. Water from the rock: Exod.
xvii. 1–7, verses 3–6 are E.

47.   Sinai: Exod. xix., xxiv., xxxii. 1 to xxxiv. 28,
with E's legal code in xx.–xxiii.
xxxiv. 29 to the end of the book is P.

48.   'The law our schoolmaster. . . . ': Gal iii. 24.
The JE narrative of the wanderings is resumed
in Num. x. 29.

Page
49.   The story of the spies is in Num. xiii. and xiv.,
        mostly JE.
        Avoidance of Edom: Num. xx. 14–21.
        Story of Balaam: Num. xxii. 2 to xxiv.–end,
        all J and E.
50.   Passing of Moses: Deut. xxxiv. 1–6, JE.
        'The exodus which *He* should accomplish . . . . ':
        S. Luke ix. 30, 31.   Greek *exodos* translated
        decease, which has same literal meaning of
        Way out or Departure.

Chapter VII

FROM THE SETTLEMENT OF CANAAN TO THE DIVISION OF THE KINGDOM

51.   Israel called Jahveh's first-born son: Exod. iv.
        22, 23 J, cp. Hos. xi. 1.
        Jahveh the Shepherd of Israel: Ps. lxxx. 1,
        xxiii. 1, etc., cp. Isa. xl. 11.
        The Ark at Jordan: JE story is Josh. iii. 1, 5,
        10 to iv. 11, 15–18.
        The Ark at Jericho: JE story is Josh. v. 13
        to vi. 27.

In support of this view note (i) that the name Asher occurs in the
16th century B.C. in the precise locality which Biblical tradition allots
to that tribe at the Settlement.   (ii.) The unfriendly behaviour of
Asher and Dan in Judges v. 21.

52.   Cereal offerings: Exod. xxii. 29, xxiii. 19 E,
        Judges vi. 19, xiii. 23, etc.
        Agricultural feasts:—
            (1) Firstfruits, combined with ⎫
                Passover   ⎪
            (2) Weeks, conclusion of   ⎬ Exod. xxiii.
                wheat harvest   ⎪ 14–17 E.
            (3) Ingathering, rest of pro- ⎭
                duce
        Sabbath: See references to last chapter.
        Nazirites (probably = consecrated ones), Judge
        xiii. 3–5, cp. Amos ii. 12.
        P legislation in Num. vi.

CHAPTER VIII

ISRAEL AND JUDAH

[NOTE.—Detailed references to the prophets are
not given. The best way to study one of

Page

these books is first to ascertain its historical
context and then to read it straight through.
After that, consult a simple commentary as to
its composition, divisions, etc. and read it
again in the light of that information.]

63.   Uzziah, king of Judah: 2 Kings xiv. 21, cp.
2 Chron. xxv. 25 to xxvi. 23.
[NOTE.—Chronicles belongs at earliest to the
second half of the fourth century, and is therefore much later than Kings.]
Call of Isaiah: Isa. vi.
Reign of Ahaz in Judah: 2 Kings xvi.

63.   Reign of Hezekiah in Judah: 2 Kings xviii.–xx.
63, 64.   Fall of Samaria and origin of Samaritans:
2 Kings xvii.
64.   Doctrine of the remnant: 2 Kings xix. 31,
Isa. iv. 2–6, x. 20, etc.
The rod from the stem of Jesse: Isa. xi. 1–10.

65.   Reigns of Manasseh and Amon: 2 Kings xxi., cp.
2 Chron. xxxiii. and 'Prayer of Manasseh.'
Reign of Josiah: 2 Kings xxii. 1 to xxiii. 30.

66.   Call of Jeremiah: Jer. i. 4–12.
66, 67.   Deuteronomy: law of love, vii. 6–11, etc.
one sanctuary, xii. 1–14, etc.

68, 69.   Fall of Jerusalem in 597: 2 Kings xxiii. 31 to
xxv. 7, cp. Jer. xxxix.
69.   Jeremiah's vision of the figs: Jer. xxiv., cp.
Ezek. viii.
Legend about the Ark: 2 Macc. ii. 1–8.

CHAPTER IX

EXILE, RETURN AND RESTORATION

70.   Homesickness of exiles: Ps. cxxxvii.
71.   Ezekiel, vision of the Chariot of God: Ezek. i.–iii.
Acted prophecies of destruction of Jerusalem:
Ch. iv. 1 to v. 4.

The following tables may be useful for this and the following chapter:—

A. THE SYRIAN KINGS

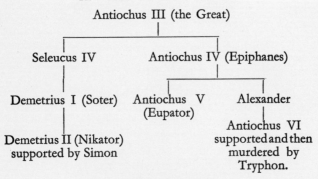

Antiochus III (the Great)

Seleucus IV

Antiochus IV (Epiphanes)

Demetrius I (Soter)

Antiochus V (Eupator)

Alexander

Demetrius II (Nikator) supported by Simon

Antiochus VI supported and then murdered by Tryphon.

B. THE MACCABEES

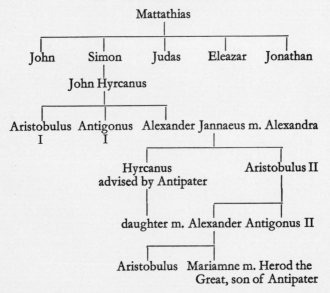

Mattathias

John   Simon   Judas   Eleazar   Jonathan

John Hyrcanus

Aristobulus I   Antigonus I   Alexander Jannaeus m. Alexandra

Hyrcanus advised by Antipater

Aristobulus II

daughter m. Alexander   Antigonus II

Aristobulus   Mariamne m. Herod the Great, son of Antipater

NOTE.—II Maccabees is a later and quite independent narrative of the history from the time of Seleucus IV (187–176 B.C.) to the defeat of Nicanor in 161.

Page

109.　'If ye love Me, ye will keep . . . ': John xiv. 15.
'Ye are My friends, if ye do . . . ': John xv. 14.

The Kingdom of Heaven: Matt. xiii. [New righteousness that goes with it: Matt. v.–vii.]
The 'Strong Man' passage: Mark iii. 22–27, Matt. xii. 22–29, Luke xi. 14–22, cp. Isa. xlix. 24–26.

111.　Feeding of the Five Thousand: Mark vi. 30–44, Matt. xiv. 13–21, Luke ix. 10–17, John vi. (with discourse following).
S. Peter's Confession and First Prediction of the Passion: Mark viii. 27 to ix. 1, Matt. xvi. 13–28, Luke ix. 18–27.
The account of the Transfiguration follows immediately in each of the Synoptic Gospels.

112.　'Set His face steadfastly . . . ': Luke ix. 51, cp. Isa. l. 7.

113.　Triumphal entry: Mark xi. 1–10, Matt. xxi. 1–9, Luke xix. 29–38, John xii. 12–15.

CHAPTER XV

THE PASSION

115ff.　Thursday evening: Mark xiv. 12–26, Matt. xxvi. 17–30, Luke xxii. 7–23, cp. John xiii. to xvii. and 1 Cor. xi. 23ff.

118.　*Tetelestai:* John xix. 30.
119.　Rending of the veil: Mark xv. 38.

CHAPTER XVI

THE RESURRECTION AND ASCENSION

122ff.　Narratives of the Great Forty Days: Mark xvi. 1–8 (+ 9–20), Matt. xxviii., Luke xxiv. + Acts i. 1–11, John xx. and xxi., 1 Cor. xv. 1–11.

130.　The five sayings: Matt. xxviii. 19 and 20, Acts i. 4, 8 and 11.

Chapter XVII

BIRTH AND EQUIPMENT OF THE CHURCH

Chapter XVIII

THE CHURCH'S GROWTH TO MATURITY

Page
151.   From the Definition of Chalcedon:—

'Following therefore the holy fathers, we all teach, with one accord, one and the same Son, our Lord Jesus Christ. . . . Who for us men and for our salvation, according to the manhood, was born of the Virgin Mary, the God-bearer, one and the same Christ, Son, Lord,—only-begotten, confessed in two natures, without confusion, without change, without division or separation. The difference of the natures is in no way denied by reason of their union: on the other hand, the peculiarity of each nature is preserved and both concur in one Person and one hypostasis.' The translation is Dr. Kidd's.

CHAPTER XXIII

THE UNFULFILLED PROPHECIES

186ff.   The Second Coming, and events preceding and following: S. Mark xiii. and parallels, cp. Luke xviii. 8, 1 Thess. iv. 13 to v. 3, 2 Thess. i. 7 to ii. 12, 2 Cor. v. 10, cp. Rev. i. 7, 1 John ii. 18ff, 2 John 7.

Our Lord's teaching on the resurrection in the Fourth Gospel: John v. 19–29, vi. 26–58.

S. Paul's analogy of the corn: 1 Cor. xv., cp. John xii. 24.

190.   Millennium passage: Rev. xx.

192.   Parable of sheep and goats: Matt. xxv. 31–46.
Parable of the Servants: Luke xii. 35–48.

194.   Gehenna passage in S. Mark: Mark ix. 42–50, cp. Isa. lxvi. 24.

The New Jerusalem: Rev. xxi. 1 to xxii. 5.

P

NOTES ON THE TAILPIECES

These notes are put here instead of under the pictures, so that those to whom such detailed symbolism does not appeal can leave them unread!

The tailpieces are in three sets of four, each bearing on one of the three metaphorical illustrations which run through the book, namely the Mountain, the Bridge and the Ship. For the passages in the text, consult the Index.

THE MOUNTAIN

I. PAGE 22. Man, "very good" as he was created, stands at the outset of his development facing the straight path of progress which God intended for him. A member of the lower creation stands beside him, for its future is bound up with his.

II. PAGE 30. Man has turned aside from the straight path and landed himself in a *cul-de-sac* from which there is no exit. Estranged from God and arrested in their development, men are at variance both with each other and with the beasts. The detail is difficult to see amid the general chaos, but besides the hunters and the woman fallen into a Slough of Despond on the right, very sharp eyes will discern a monkey stealing a baby and a hunted hare on the left, and above the woman, terrible eyes glaring from the thicket,—symbol of the *fear* that dominates the life of man apart from God. Note also the thicket closing over the untrodden highway; the lamb, itself innocent, turning to join the rest of creation on the wrong road; and the mourning angels above.

III. PAGE 113. The Second Adam, enabled by the Holy Spirit, is treading the Way of Holiness from which the first turned aside, and breasting through the thicket that has overgrown it. The snake at His heel recalls both Gen. iii. 15 and the Messianic psalm xci. 13; while the rabbit and the swallow following up the cleared path remind you that the whole creation is to be included in the Restoration, as it was in the Fall.* On the left is the lily among thorns of Cant. ii. 2, which points the fact that all life which moves Godward in this world does so *by means of* the pains and limitations which encompass it.

IV. PAGE 121. "From His poor manger"—see the stable at the foot of the hill,—"to His bitter Cross" the Second Adam has trodden the Way of Holiness entire. By so doing He has opened a road from the *cul-de-sac* also to the top,—a winding road indeed, but one that most surely gets there. The triumphant Sixth Word, the golden *Tetelestai*, is written in Greek capitals against the perfect rainbow that symbolizes both the faithfulness of God and the completeness of the Atonement wrought by the Second Adam between Him and man. There was no room to draw figures on this small picture; but you must imagine the captives in the *cul-de-sac* gazing with wonder at the newly opened way, and beginning to press along it.

THE BRIDGE

I. PAGE 36. The gulf yawns between God and fallen man, but the Bridge is already in building, and it is God and man from opposite sides who are building it. The front figure on the left,—the human side,—is faithful Abraham, and others of his seed are following.

II. PAGE 80. The Bridge, which has advanced a long way since the time of Abraham, is being built now by the faithful remnant of Israel in their character of Suffering Servant of Jahveh. The men at the end of the Bridge are jeering and throwing stones, and the Servant is *using the stones* to build the Bridge. Note that the other side of the Bridge is hidden in cloud: the Servant, like his Divine prototype in Gethsemane and on the Cross, walks

---

* Cp. 1 John ii. 2, where the word translated world is *cosmos* or universe; and Rom. viii. 19-22. It is related that when Luther had finished his commentary on this great chapter, he turned to his dog and exclaimed rapturously, "Thou too shalt have a little golden tail!"

not by sight but by faith, believing *in* God when all sense of His love and guidance is withdrawn.

III. PAGE 97. Here is the Bridge at the supreme moment of the Incarnation. By the obedience of Mary and the operation of the Holy Ghost the Keystone is coming to its place. The Bridge *is* a Bridge at last, though not yet quite ready to be walked over; and He Who links the two sides is Himself both God and man.

IV. PAGE 131. The Bridge is finished and in use. In the middle is the Keystone, marked with the Cross that fixed it there for ever, firm and immutable. He Who has overcome the sharpness of death waits to lead all believers into the Kingdom of Heaven; and a representative throng of modern people are starting on their way. The child is running on ahead, because it is only by becoming as little children that any can enter the Kingdom. The lamb represents the lower creation sharing in the Restoration.

THE SHIP

I. PAGE 139. The fishing-smack of Pentecost, which is the infant Church, sets out from the quay of Judaism, where she was built, on her age-long voyage. Her nets are spread and straining already with the haul. There are rocks ahead and she has no chart or time-table on board, but the Holy Dove who hovers above her is guarantee that she will reach her goal.

II. PAGE 176. The Ship of the Church has grown since Pentecost, but she has also lost her unity. Instead of an open fishing-boat, we have a two-decker, with no commerce between the decks of East and West, and a number of smaller craft alongside whose occupants are busy protesting both at the Ship and at each other. Yet both Ship and boats are still on the same course, and still guided by the Holy Spirit, though the way is very rough and rocky.

III. PAGE 185. Here you must think of the middle deck, which represents Ecclesia Anglicana, as having a little open piece in front, which is all that appears in this picture. On it stand a few representative English people, some looking out over the sea towards their journey's end, others thinking nothing at all about it.   Below them on the lower deck the Roman Catholics, above them the Holy Orthodox, around them the Protestants in the boats, are similarly diversely occupied; only the souls in Paradise, represented here as in the previous and following pictures by the seabirds that follow the Ship, all have their eyes fixed on the goal.   But they are all approaching it none the less.

IV. PAGE 196.   Here is the end of the voyage and the consummation of God's loving purpose.   The last great storm of earth has washed the Ship of the Church into the port of Heaven.   Her passengers, disembarking on the quay, are about to troop up through the gates into the City.   It has been a near thing for some, but even they, "some on planks and some on things of the Ship,"*—or maybe of the boats,—are being helped ashore, where there are no tears nor death, nor mourning nor crying nor pain, any more.†   The three Hebrew letters written below (from right to left, āleph, mēm, nūn, *'mn*) are the consonants of the root referred to on p. 10, from which come both *'amen*, truly, and *'emeth*, truth, and which means to be firm, dependable.   *For faithful is He who calleth us, Who also will do it.*

* Acts xxvii. 44.   † Rev. xxi. 4.

INDEX

17p62 Religion is faith issuing in Conduct.

113   Hosanna = Save Now.

110   Redemption proceeds from Gods Holiness.

111   3 Events before Passion; Feeding 5000
                                2 Peters Confession
                                3 Transfiguration

105   2nd Adam tempted in ⎰ Faith –
                        ⎱ Love –
                        ⎱ Obedience.

112   Transfiguration Luke – Moses & Elijah – Xts Exodus at Jerus